S.O.S

SOLUTION OF SIMPLICITY

BY

T.C. BROTHERS

SIMPLYTC & CO.
NEW YORK, NEW YORK

THIS IS A BOOK OF HEALING

ISBN: 978-0-9907039-0-7

Cover Design Kevin Bines
Book Design SimpyTC & Co.

SimplyTC & Co.
SimplyTC1969@gmail.com
www.solutionofsimplicity.com

New York, New York

DEDICATION

Dedicated to Edwin C. Brothers
"Pop"

TABLE OF CONTENTS

ACKNOWLEDGEMENTS

Thanks to all who made a difference.
Thanks to my Higher Power (Love).

PREFACE

In 2005 my addiction hit an all-time high while I hit an all-time low. As I found myself in a treatment facility, with pen in hand, I was determined to document it all; the lessons learned, the feelings felt, and what did and did not work for me. When asked by a counselor why I was always writing, I said: *"If I can help just one person with my experience, then my whole addiction would not have been in vain."* This book was born of the eight hand-written journals that followed.

Solution of Simplicity is the simple solution we have all been hoping for. It can be, if we are willing, the answer to every last one of our destructive behaviors. In less than 150 pages, I have outlined a very real solution to a problem that until now has been unable to be solved; ourselves. SOS provides the key to opening a door that's been a-long-time-closed and deadlocked. The repetition within these pages is very deliberate. SOS is not an overnight fix but a new honest willingness (found only within ourselves) to practice a very new and different way of thinking, reacting, and living. After all, our old way surely has not worked.

- TC Brothers

This is a course in freedom from active addiction, please take notes.

"Had you not lacked faith that it could be solved, the problem would be gone." - A Course In Miracles

Addiction is extremely complicated. Recovery is simple.

CHAPTER I

IT'S LONELY AT THE BOTTOM

Look past the weather beaten clothes and the street torn shoes. Can you see past the dirty face, the greasy hair, the unbrushed teeth? Can you see as far as the eyes? It is in the eyes where we remember. It is here where we recognize something we know we once knew. It is in the eyes that you will recognize your brother, and it is in his eyes that you will find or lose yourself.

Do not pity this man and do not judge him either. Reach out your hand, he just may take hold. Throw him a rope, he's not too far gone. Talk to him like he's a human being, because that is what he is. Let him know, that which you are offering is genuine, because love can be nothing but. I tell you now, he feels alone, and even though he let you catch a glimpse of his soul by letting you see his eyes, if only for an instant, it is only because he wants help.

Do not look down on this man because he cannot look you directly in the eye for more than that instant. He truly believes all the hateful lies his sick mind has been telling him. Like millions of active addicts around the globe, this man is sick, but there is a way to get better. There is a way to be free.

This man does not want your pity, and he does not want your charity. Although, he will likely accept some charity from time to time because addiction deprives, and he believes he is forced to,

But in reality, all he really needs is some guidance, some hope, someone to look him right in the eye and talk to him like he is a person. He doesn't need an authority figure talking down at him, telling him what he needs to do, or what he should have done. The ruthless punisher that lives in his head has been screaming this at him for years. Maybe he wants to look at you and think: "Somebody really does care." Maybe he just needs an understanding friend to talk to, or something as simple as a hug.

Maybe he is a man, who was once a child, a child who just wanted to fit in, and because he believed what this strange world was showing him, grew into a misguided teenager. Maybe he was a teenager, who because of a few unfortunate turns of events in his life, fell in with the wrong crowd. Before he knew it, he was pretending he was something he wasn't, and well on his way to being hooked on that lie. It seems like this teenager never really stood a chance. In a blink of an eye, he found himself in his late twenties, working yet another dead end job that he could barely show up for, trying to support a small family, and all the while trying to keep that lie alive. Knowing in his heart, however, that sooner or later, it was all bound to come crashing down on him. It had to. It always does.

Maybe he is a man who, convinced by the voice that haunts him, believes that his children would be better off without him. Maybe he really does want to change, but because of how many times he has tried to no avail, has given up hope. Show compassion for this man. He truly believes the world would be a better place if he would just go crawl into a hole and die, so he tries to do just that. The problem is, when he crawls into his hole, instead of dying like he wishes, his phone stops ringing, his friends disappear and he finds himself addicted and alone, teetering on the brink of insanity, and wondering where everybody went.

Maybe he doesn't want to hurt anymore, and maybe he is sick of hurting others as well. Maybe he is tired of that old familiar look of disappointment on the faces of everyone who ever meant anything to him in his whole, miserable lifetime. Maybe he is just like us, just like me who is writing this, and just like you who is reading it. Maybe he is your brother, your sister, your mother, or your father, for addiction touches us all. This is what I'm here to remind you, and at the same time I am reminding myself: He is me. She is us.

Addiction is a part of our life that most of us, when coming into recovery, would rather put behind us and forget all together. But we mustn't just yet. Dishonesty and denial is what brought us to rock bottom and if we continue in our denial, we are bound to keep on repeating the same mistakes that have led us to a life of insane addiction. We have now come to a point where this will not do.

It's hard to breathe down there at the bottom;
it's hard to think straight and see straight.

The bottom is lonely. The bottom is cold. And it doesn't matter if you're in a stadium filled with 60,000 people, or at a party with a few friends, when you're at the bottom; the bed is empty no matter who lays beside you. The bottom is a hard place. It is a dark place, and if you think you've got it bad now, wait and see where you will end up if you continue this insane and unhealthy lifestyle of active addiction, dishonesty and denial.

The bottom is insanity. Self-abuse of any kind is insane. The bottom is as far from God as one could get; yet when I finally crashed at my bottom, I found myself closer to God than I had ever been before. Many of us cringe when we hear the word God but let me assure you; this book is not trying to make you believe in anything that does not agree with your heart.

For many years I was caught in the confines of my addiction, and I was experiencing all the side effects that came along with it: The failures, the disappointments and the instability. I was infected with poison and I brought my toxic cloud with me wherever I went. If our paths crossed, you crossed paths with my disease. During this time, I barely gave hurting someone a second thought. It wasn't that I didn't care, I was just completely unaware. I would always act first and deal with the consequences later.

I never intended to hurt anyone, well, except for myself.

In active addiction, the good times in life are always short lived.

The destruction in the wake of this insanity carries with it a dark cloud of paranoia, and for me, in its advanced stage, detailed thoughts of suicide. My life became consumed by these thoughts, in conjunction with the never ending nagging of an overly active addiction, which was always hungry and aching to be fed.

My mental and physical health was deteriorating fast. I couldn't tell anyone how sick I was, because I would not allow myself to trust anyone. I could no longer look at myself in the mirror or my children in their eyes. Here I would stay for two more long years, and they were the longest two years of my life. The unwell voice in my one track mind had me convinced that it was too late and that I would go to my grave a struggling, suffering addict. This was not supposed to happen. This is not what I signed up for. I was not supposed to get hooked. Or was I?

As my addiction progressed so did the insanity. I no longer wanted to abuse myself, but was doing so against my will. I was a slave and something had to give.

Although a chemically obscured vision might seem very real because of the intense emotion connected to it, a life seen through the eyes of an active addict is as far from reality as one can get. Our knowledge of the real truth becomes covered like a casket, and every dirty little lie we tell, is yet another shovel filled with soil carelessly thrown on top. Plus, our denial has us convinced that the crabgrass that grows on the cold ground above is a plush lawn of Kentucky Blue.

Denial is powerful. Denial is deadly. Suicide is NOT the Solution.

There was this reoccurring daydream I would have from time to time, where in a miraculous moment I would break free from the chains that held me. I imagined what it would feel like to be free. However, the daydream was always short lived thanks to that old familiar thought in my head that kept loudly insisting that it was too late, and that I was way too far gone. What a mess!

The image I had deliberately constructed to face the world, throughout my lifetime no longer served me and the pain became so great, that I had become willing to let this image go entirely. I had to come clean, or else...

HELP!!!

I have been lying. I am not okay and everything is not fine. I don't want to live like this anymore and I don't want to die. I desperately need help! I can't do it alone and I'm tired of trying. Please?

When I asked for help, help is what I got. I found out very quickly that contrary to what my previous thoughts would have me believe, it was certainly NOT too late to change my life. It is never too late to start thinking right and living healthy. I realized there were indeed two voices within my mind, and for years, I'd only been able to hear one; the voice that hated me and pointed to all the shit in the world. Since then, I've come to find there is another voice: The voice that loves me, and points to all that is good and beautiful in this world. This is the voice we have drowned out with the insanity of our active addiction. However, with dedication and practice, we will hear this voice of wisdom more clearly and more often than ever before.

Even if I die tomorrow, I am determined to live this day right.

From this day forward, we will attempt living life with as much integrity as possible. This is something we have never tried before, which leads us to believe it may work! With the simple decision to be honest comes the instant relief of no longer having to remember

7

all those lies. All the energy we've wasted keeping those lies alive is no longer being spent. This allows our restless mind to simmer down to an almost motionless pond. Peace is now able to be recognized, where it has always been, beyond the mayhem in our mind. This peace belongs to us all. All we have to do is claim it, accept it, and continue to nurture it.

What we're addicted to does not matter.
A life out of control is a life out of control.

It can be money or it can be honey; too much of anything is what causes unmanageability, and if not caught early, total loss of control over one's own life.

The simple solution you hold in your heart. However, in order to utilize this, you must choose to stop listening to what the unhealthy voice has been telling you. It is this judging and unforgiving voice that will keep you in chains. This is the voice that has brought you to the madness of bottom, and it is surely this voice that will keep you there.

In order to start hearing the other voice, the healthy voice, the voice within our heart, we must quiet our unruly mind. For the gentle voice of the heart, is as consistent in tone as it is in its message. It will never try and be heard over the merciless noise that is already going on in your head. Occasionally, in active addiction, you may receive a glimpse of what the heart is trying to say, but only a glimpse. There is so much more waiting to reveal itself to you if you are willing to receive it. Consistently practice quieting your mind and hear the unfailing message beyond it. It is the unchanging sureness, beyond the chaotic mayhem, that is going to guide you throughout this process and through the rest of your life in recovery. Make the decision to practice. The more you practice, the more serene your mind will become and the more you will be able to receive the heart's guidance. Suddenly, you will realize that you are spending less time suffering, and more time at peace.

Many refer to the hateful voice in their head as the disease of addiction, while others call it insanity. However, it does not matter which label you assign to it, this unhealthy voice is just that of the ego and the ego ultimately wants to assassinate its host.

This ruthless and unforgiving voice within our mind is the painful reality that we have been trying to avoid. In doing so, we have come to find ourselves addicted and more lost than ever before. It's time to try another way to get healthy and clean because our old way obviously did not work. After all we've been through; it is good to know that there is another way.

When we start abusing ourselves with a substance, whether we are aware of it yet or not, we were trying to avoid something. Some call it life, some call it truth, and others call it self. And the more we run from ourselves, the further we fall from reality. In active addiction, we all soon reach a point where we feel only pain and emptiness. This suffering is what keeps us trying to maintain a numbness that is literally unmaintainable.

Although we may think we *hate our life* while trapped at our bottom, in truth we do not hate life *but fear living.*

A life of active addiction is not living at all, but in fact, the avoidance of life. If we want to proceed in recovery rather than illness, we must do so with a clear head and sober eyes. You must lay down your method of destruction right now.

Fear seems real but I assure you it is not. You will come to know this as you walk through enough of your own. There is nothing to fear in this process and this is reality.

Through sober eyes you will see a new world. You will have a greater understanding of what truth is. You will also understand that truth has always been with you because wherever you go, your heart goes there too. No matter how fast you run, or how far, no matter where you hide, or how well, truth is always bound to catch up.

**No matter how far I ran or how numb I got,
I was always there when I returned.**

When the numbness wears off, truth catches up. Stop running and truth will find you. Truth is not illusive but unavoidable. Truth is reality. Untruth is not.

All of that running and hiding, all of those well crafted lies, and where did I end up? At death's door, face to face with the truth, yet still convinced by the lie. It wasn't until I was cornered by death that I found the will to live. Indeed it was here, at my lowest bottom, that I met God.

THE BEGINNING OF THE END

When the old me left, the new me arrived.

It was at death's door that I found new life. It was at death's door that I decided to surrender the struggle and fight for my life. It was at death's door I realized I did not want to die. The illusion of death pushed me towards life. And the lie that I was living, pushed me directly into the awareness of truth. In that moment, I went from total terror, to perfect peace. When I made the decision to live, I knew deep in my soul that this time, it would be different.

My suffering had reached its boiling point. At this point, nothing mattered but saving my life. It was in this moment of surrender that the old me died, and a new me was born. Death gave way to new life. Just like the butterfly that emerges from her cocoon to take flight for the very first time. Life in the womb ends when the baby is born into this world and takes its very first bittersweet breath.

With our new life before us, we must set out to learn all we can about recovering. What will we do in this next chapter of life? To forget and fall back into the unawareness is no longer an option. We have barely given ourselves a chance here, but now, we intend to.

When is the last time you have given yourself a real chance?

We can recreate our life right here and now, in honesty and with good health in focus. Through surrender we let go of all our old addictive attachments and insane behaviors. In doing so, we are introduced to a freedom long since forgotten. Near death has given us new life, and what is born into this life anew, indeed is the death of the old. I am thankful that this is not the end, but only a new beginning.

ONE WAR STORY

It was bad right from the start.

I remember back to the very beginning of the insanity, back when I was very young. I was at a house party with a bunch of people who claimed to be friends. Not yet knowing my limit, I drank way more than I should have. I vaguely remember a couple of my friends directing me to a nearby park. I can remember hearing them laughing while I kneeled at the foot of a nearby tree, vomiting violently. I remember the feeling of cold wet jeans against my knees and the smell of blackberry vomit in the crisp winter air. I remember their laughter fading as they got further away, leaving me there to fend for myself. I remember crying and yelling and cursing and vomiting. I set off on the long walk towards home. I was trying to make sense of what happened; Where'd everybody go? Where are all of my friends when I need them? I heard a familiar horn honking behind me and turned to face the blaring headlights of my Dad's 1976 Chevy Van. I remember climbing into the van and the disbelief in my father's voice. My little brother didn't say a word.

I remember feeling separate from everything. I remember my mother's hysterics. I remember lying on the bathroom floor and throwing up. This was the night I lost touch with God. I remember how I felt the next morning; guilty and empty. I swore I would never drink again.

I remember going to school on Monday. It seemed everyone was talking about me. Welcomed by a wall of cold shoulders and sarcasm, I felt I was truly on my own. This is when the insanity took hold of my life and made me promises that, compared to what I was feeling at the time, sounded pretty damn good. I easily fell for the lie. I believed in it early. I didn't like the way life felt, and I didn't want to feel anymore. Goodbye Sanity…

A MOMENT OF CLARITY

After years of listening to the voice in my head that hated me, one night I heard a very different voice within me. A calming voice and when it spoke, I knew that it was true. It said, very quietly and very clearly, "You are not supposed to die at the hands of this disease; This is not the plan." And every once in awhile this loving voice would catch me off guard, in a moment of clarity, and tell me to "Ask for help." I actually started to entertain this crazy idea. Was getting help really possible? But then thanks again to my logical denial, back to the bottom I sank.

WE CHOOSE OUR BOTTOM

Getting high, no matter what our method, quickly converts into a painful chore. They call it getting high, but it has taken us lower than we ever thought we would go. The only thing good about hitting rock bottom is the knowing that once you arrive at this cold lonely place, you have indeed reached what could be a turning point. Since everyone's bottom is different, only you can decide how low you are actually willing to go, and how long you are actually willing to stay. There is great freedom in knowing we choose our own bottom; although I was unaware of this while trapped in my active addiction. I was convinced, like many of you are now, that I was at the mercy of my insane addiction, and thought I was a victim of the world that surrounded me. Once again I was wrong.

Denial is addiction at its most awful.
Denial says there's no need for change. Denial pretends there is

no problem. Denial is our disease at its most powerful. And when we are in denial, we are unaware that what was supposed to bring us some sort of pleasure or escape is what is actually keeping us tied and bound. Denial is one of the roots of much of our pain.

Denial will keep you hovering somewhere just above bottom until the suffering becomes too much to take. The suffering ends when we say it ends. And anytime we slip back into forgetfulness and find ourselves suffering again, we can simply choose to be honest again. It truly is this simple.

As I hovered right above bottom, I considered myself worthless. I no longer wanted to live, and I truly believed in nothing, not even myself. I sure could talk a good game out in the world though. I would impress many with my well rehearsed fabrications. My fine polished façade would be delivered with such confidence and pin-point accuracy, that even I would walk away from the one sided conversation convinced. I had mastered the art of manipulation to the point that it had become very dangerous to my own health.

When we become such a master of manipulation,
that we start believing our own lies,
are we really the master, or are we just fools?

When we believe our lies, we will fight to defend them. Soon we find ourselves living to cover them up. Trying to keep track of who was told what, and when, and where, eventually becomes a big tangled mess and just another part of the chaotic mayhem that is the life of the active addict. Manipulated truth is NOT truth. Therefore, you must stop defending it now.

Be willing to maintain urgent self honesty and the
complicated lie you've concocted will fall away to dust.
Simply stop defending the lie and it dies.

HOPELESS NOT HELPLESS

I was hopeless because I believed I couldn't be helped. However, all who are willing to be helped will be helped.

Not knowing if I was coming or going and looking at suicide as a feasible solution, I wasn't sure of anything anymore. I was enslaved by a substance and living a life without any substance. I was exhausted and just about ready to give up. The notion that we would consider suicide before reaching out for help is proof that there is something very wrong in the mind of the active addict. The return to Sanity requires this recognition.

The more I suffered, the more attractive death became. The more I self medicated in order to stop suffering, the more I suffered. Addiction is a sick cycle affecting not only the addict and the addict's family, but friends, acquaintances, strangers, and society as a whole. Many times I'd think to myself What do they care? I am not hurting anyone but myself. I was also very wrong about this.

If you are an active addict reading this, and you think you are only hurting yourself, there are a few things you must consider: You are not, and have not, been thinking clearly. You will not be able to think clearly, until you get a little time without poison in your bloodstream. Even the things you think you see with your own two eyes are seen through the veil of insane, active addiction. The addict's perception is warped and his illusions have him fooled.

Recovery is possible but you cannot recover alone.

There may still be a thought in your mind that thinks you do not need anyone. Your disease would love to trap you into a few more years, or even lifetimes, of attempting to recover on your own. Remember, you are not thinking clearly. Do not let your addiction fool you again.

Avoiding our problems will only work momentarily. Attempting to stay numb will only cover up our problems until the anesthesia stops working. We are then left with a lifetime's worth of covered up problems. Identifying with our suffering is unhealthy and extremely painful. However, this is the pain that brings change. Burying a problem only assures us one thing, that indeed the problem is still there. Untruth need only be uncovered and looked at correctly if it is to be seen as it truly is and let go. Trying to keep a problem hidden so that no one suspects that there is one, is mad.

The last thing my diseased ego wanted me to do was admit that I could have been wrong. In fact, it was ready to bring me to my grave in order to prove that it was right. I desperately needed help. Our closed minded illness would rather us go to an early grave, than admit that we could have been wrong. Today, I take a solid strike against my insane disease and freely admit; I can be wrong, I have been wrong, and I will without question be wrong again! Addiction will bring us to an early grave if we let it. Denial ends where open minded self-honesty begins.

INNER GUIDANCE

Maybe you're not 20 years into an addiction that has left you hopeless and suicidal. Maybe it is something else that has you unhappy. Maybe it's just an uneasy feeling deep down in the pit of your stomach that is telling you something just isn't right. You can listen to your *Inner Guidance* now, or you can listen to it many years from now, but eventually, we all have to hear it. We can only drown out truth for so long until whatever it is we are using to try and drown it out, no longer works for us. Eventually our sedative will wear off, and we will have to deal with that which we've been avoiding all along. Yes, eventually, we will all have to face our Self.

I am no longer asking myself; What's the use? I am no longer having daily thoughts of suicide, and I am no longer abusing myself with substances and insane behavior. I no longer feel sick to my stomach when I look in the mirror. I sleep easy at night and breathe easy during the day. Some days I am actually able to look in the mirror and smile, while other days I still momentarily forget to forgive what stares back at me. However, with practice I am able to look upon myself with compassion, and this is a long stretch from the punishment endured down there at the bottom. Sure, I still wake up in the morning and feel a little off center sometimes, but even on the hard days, there is an underlying thankfulness for how far I've come, and where I now stand.

From here, I am reaching out to you. Grab hold!

We've spent enough time abusing ourselves. Now it is time we take care of ourselves.

If we want to continue to receive help, we must continue to ask for it and accept it when it comes. Asking for help was a fantasy of mine, long before it became my reality. I became exhausted from years of pretending everything was fine when it wasn't. Living the lie of addiction will drain you of all that is good. I remember wanting to get honest the very next time someone would ask me how I was doing.

We all have our triggers. Today, instead of bringing me back to where I don't want to be, these triggers are simply reminders of where I don't want to be. I was living a nightmare and my spirit was wounded. I felt like I was on my own; just another forgotten tragedy; left all alone and sentenced to death. However, I was wrong about this. With a foundation of self-honesty, the chances of falling back into our old insane ways for any lengthy amount of time are diminishing. Today our spirit thanks us.

HEALTHY MIND HEALTHY LIFE

Our health must always come first because without it, we are no good to anyone.

When it comes to recovery you must be selfish. Your recovery is about you. It is about your health. It's about your life. How can you be good to anyone else, if you are not first good to yourself?

We have finally put our addiction aside, and recovery has taken its place.

We will now only entertain thoughts of good health and healing. We are now able to take a step back and see the world for what it really is. (A bunch of silly little dramatic situations, played out on a spinning blue ball, as it hurdles through space!) Seeing the world in this light makes it simple to let it all go. In giving up trying to control, we actually regain control of our lives, and the world will dictate no more. With practice, we will be able to stop and think before we react to the little situations on life's shallow surface. We will no longer allow any situation to decide for us, who we are. How we react is always our choice, and our choices dictate our life.

Breaking the bad habit of *reacting first* takes work. We have to re-train ourselves to stop and think first. It does not matter what the situation is, learning to stop and think first is a crucial step in early recovery. When we react without thinking first, the reaction is usually unhealthy.

This bad habit is on its way out.

We must take ourselves off autopilot. We must take full responsibility for the situation we now find ourselves in. We must take responsibility for our past if we are to be free of it. Once we stop using excuses and blame, we become responsible for the mess we have made of our life. Only then will the answer become apparent. There is no justification for unhealthy behavior, and blame will only prolong the healing process.

With focus and commitment to a new way of life, we become occupied and are able to momentarily step out of the insanity that has held us prisoner for so long. Indeed we want to spend more time here.

And so we begin down this path towards Sanity.

To become a master of anything, devoted practice is required. Just as we had to keep repeating the same insanity to become insane, we must keep repeating the same sanity over and over again in order to remain sane. Repetition in this area is key. Eventually, what we practice will become so automatic that we will no longer require as much practice at all.

No longer trapped in an insane world, we will begin living our life for the first time in a long time. Our feelings of guilt will eventually dissipate, and this amazing journey will inspire us to be what we were always meant to be. We can use this new found inspiration to create the world anew.

INSPIRATION FROM AN EMPTY SEAT

Once in very early recovery I was out for a drive when; in a moment of despair I began asking questions to the silence that rode along with me. Suddenly, while on this aimless tour of winding backstreets in the town I grew up in, I began getting answers. These answers seemed to be coming from nowhere. I was somewhat shocked as they surfaced because they seemed so familiar. My response to each answer as it came to me was; *"Of course!"*

A sudden outpouring of wisdom and self-compassion began to flood the car as my headlights pierced the night engulfed street. I knew that what I was receiving here was as close to truth as I'd ever been. I realized that this wisdom beside me was actually the truth within me and I suddenly felt protected. Here I knew, my search for truth was over. I was side swiped with awe as my heart jumped to my throat and my eyes began to fill with tears. I began crying. But these tears were different than those before. These were not tears of suffering, but relief! I immediately knew what it meant to be grateful.

Truth was always within me. I just couldn't recognize it because it had been covered up and forgotten, hidden deep beneath my addiction. There I was, and without warning, answers that made perfect sense began to flow. These answers challenged all of my closed minded beliefs, and shined a new light on all those old obsessive and compulsive thought patterns. I now had to reevaluate everything I thought I knew before.

Do not waste anymore time looking to the outside world

for inner peace. I assure you, you will not find long term happiness at the bottom of any bottle or bag.

Recovery is possible and if you are truly willing to do whatever it takes, than it is also probable. How much recovery you receive will always come down to how willing you are to receive it. If you say you are willing to receive it, but continue to behave how you have always behaved, then you will not acquire the results you seek. To change my unhealthy behavior, I simply changed my unhealthy thoughts to those that are healthy. Be willing and you too can take the worst affliction you have ever know (your addiction) and turn it into the greatest blessing you have ever received (The ability to help someone else with your experience.) Hell does have an exit, and we've found it.

I cannot believe the nightmare is over!

Waste no more time pretending to be happy when you're not. The only thing worse than being unhappy for twenty years, is being unhappy for twenty years and a day. Decide now to make whatever changes are needed in order to be happy. Our time of wasting time is over. Once we experience a taste of what true relief feels like, in true addict form, we will want more.

Goodbye bottom, my days down here are done!

CHANGE OR DIE

Right now, nothing but saving your own life should matter. This is Surrender.

The pain you feel was sent to wake you up. There is no other reason for that pain. It is here to let you know that there is something very wrong and you had better start paying it some attention. If you are not careful in this crucial stage of early recovery, the insanity will continue and could even get worse. There is a reason you feel the way you do. I know it hurts, but it does get easier.

It is time to start living instead of dying.

Today, welcome healing and happiness, for you have hurt long enough. If I can recover, you can recover. Make the decision to start living healthy. Stick to this decision and see your life improve. Every choice you make in this moment determines how the next moment will be. If I make a bad choice today it will certainly effect tomorrow. Just as all our bad choices have brought us to our bottom, every healthy choice has a consequence as well. Some call it karma and some call it fate, but no matter what the label, it is just another case of simple cause and effect. Our unhealthy choices brought sickness; our healthy choices bring healing.

The choice between addiction and recovery is the choice between madness and Sanity. In fact, living in the grip of addiction, is not really living at all. We can embrace this new healthy way of life now, or we can choose to remain stuck until the pain gets even greater. Ultimately, the choice between addiction and recovery is the choice between living and dying.

When your soul is screaming, you had better start listening!

The longer you ignore it, the worse off you will be. I know the wheels are mercilessly turning in your head, trying to persuade you to remain where you're at; trying again to convince you that it's too late to change. Stop listening to those thoughts and start listening to what your heart is telling you. Your thinking is manic but your heart speaks the truth. It is never too late to live this day right.

Pain is a great motivator. Indeed, when the pain gets great enough, you will become willing to change. However, we can always decide before the pain becomes too great and our life spins anymore out of control than it already has. We need not waste another day suffering. All change begins with a simple change of mind.

This is the Solution.

To change your life, you have to want it above all else.

CHAPTER II

HOW WILLING ARE YOU?

Recovery is the process of healing. This healing begins with the cleansing of self. You must detoxify and dry out so that you can begin to look clearly at what really needs to be looked at. Addiction is just a symptom of our mental unrest. We want to numb ourselves. We do not want to feel, because all we feel is pain. Addiction was an attempt at avoiding this pain, and all it did was add to it.

You must stop abusing yourself in all ways, before you can begin to work on the behaviors that brought you here. For me, this meant going into a treatment facility and staying for however long the professionals thought I should be there. I turned my life over to them. My pain became so great, that I became willing to turn over all that was left of my life just to save it. I was scared, not knowing what the outcome would be or where I would end up. In the beginning, there is seemingly so much to be afraid of. These fears will all diminish.

When I finally let go of all of the resistance I had left, and decided to allow a power greater than myself (in this case the professionals at a treatment facility) to take charge, without knowing it, I was beginning to trust again. Suddenly, my unmanageable life was being managed. This trust, when remembered, will illuminate the journey toward freedom and healing. Indeed the process has already begun.

BAD HABITS

Bad habits can break, but can also be broken.

Now let us focus on what needs to be focused on: Good health and recovery. How willing are you to do what needs to be done in order to stop the insanity? Freedom is only a good choice away. Are you willing to give up the lifestyle you've been living? Are you willing to admit that you have been lying, to basically everyone, about practically everything? You cannot recover alone like you thought. Are you willing to let go of the people in your life who are less than a good influence on you? Are you willing to stop going to those places that trigger unhealthy reactions?

In recovery you will find out who your real friends are. We should be thankful for this learning. Forgive those who do not have your best interest at heart. And forgive those who think that they do, but don't. Admit to yourself again now, that your way has never worked and become willing to take some suggestions. Be willing to do whatever it takes to clean up your life; even if you think it won't work. Be willing to see this book to its conclusion.

What you now hold in your hands has been proven to work. There is nothing I will suggest here in this text that hasn't already been proven to work by me.

We must also become willing to let go of our unhealthy need to be right all the time. The fact is, being right holds no importance. It is always the ego which needs to be right, while seeking to find satisfaction in making someone else wrong. This too is addictive thinking.

In recovery we must continually put our ego aside. Any time we find ourselves struggling throughout this healing process, we should remember that we could be experiencing peace instead. How willing are you to experience peace of mind rather than what you have been experiencing? Are you willing to give up this insane need to be right, right now?

The longer we wait, the longer we suffer. We can put an end to the suffering immediately by simply letting go of our need to be right. As soon as we surrender this insane need, we freely admit that we could have been wrong. Indeed, we could have been wrong about God, the world, and ourselves, and this gives us hope!

In early recovery, any idea that affects us in a negative way must be looked at, forgiven, and surrendered as soon as possible. Even if it's a subject we think we are right about. Which is more important, being right or being happy? Just because we think we are right about something, does not mean that we are. If I am suffering in my need to be right, than how right can I actually be? Nothing is so important that we should be inclined to sacrifice our own personal peace. Quite the contrary. No-thing is that important.

What if everything you've ever thought was right, wasn't?

Our need to be right is insane and will keep us caught in the grip of our insanity. Being right is NOT important. When we no longer hold onto this need to be right, all of our resentments simply fall away. Our past is forgiven, and the relief that follows proves we are onto something real. This relief makes us aware that true relief really is possible. We could not comprehend this before, because we have tried many times to stop abusing ourselves, and failed. Now we can see that we have been wrong about yet another thing we always believed we were right about: Maybe we don't have to go to our grave struggling and suffering. Maybe we really can find freedom.

We will recover to the extent of our willingness to do so.

We admit again that we could have been wrong, and begin practicing something that has this far, remained almost alien to us, humility.

Changing your mind is allowed and even encouraged on this simple pathway towards freedom. Strict honesty is an essential component on this path. If I lie to someone and think I'm getting away with something, then I am indeed still lying to myself. We have wasted enough time in denial of our lies. Today we are looking directly at them.

You cannot take responsibility in your recovery, until you become willing to take responsibility for your addiction.

The more willing you are to practice strict honesty, the more solid your recovery's foundation. Truth is the only reliable foundation because truth is unchangeable. This means it cannot crumble. Anything we've ever changed in any way was not truth. Indeed it may have felt like truth at the time, but if it was able to be changed, it was not truth. We need to remain willing to surrender our need to be right, even about what we believe truth is. We need not be concerned with the letting go of those beliefs we believe are true, for if they are indeed 'true,' they will always remain intact.

If the choices you are living no longer serve you, simply choose again.

I was just so tired of lying and trying to remember which lie I told and to whom, that now, only truth will do. I had to surrender the whole lie. The willingness to continually practice strict self-honesty brings with it, the absolute release from the utter exhaustion of active deception.

We are finished pretending and this new found freedom feels right.

What is under the mask may not be pretty, but it is honest, and that makes it beautiful. We are no longer worried what others may think. Pretending all was well when it wasn't has been extremely draining on our spirit. The end of pretending brings forth the pure relief and renewed energy of a soul reborn. You may smile now!

POWERLESS

Life is too short to keep testing the waters of despair.

You are powerless over anyone else's recovery, except your own. No one can be willing for you, and you cannot be willing for anyone else. You cannot recover for another, no matter how much you love them. Recovery is something we must accept for ourselves. Our fear based and addicted mind-set will not give up without a fight. To resist a lie is to make it real. Simply surrender to truth, again and again, as many times as it takes and then trust that truth is inevitable.

The more we practice, the more automatic our program becomes.

The fact that you are reading these words proves without question that you have at least one small spark of hope left within you. This spark is all that is needed for a full on recovery. Feed this spark and watch it grow. Accept nothing that does not register as true within your heart, and surrender that which no longer does. The willingness to remain dedicated to truth is the decision to keep an open mind. Forgive all that needs forgiving and let it go. Do this right now, for your grudges no longer serve you.

NOTHING IS INCURABLE

Active-addiction is just a bad behavior and behaviors can be changed.

Recovery is the process of unlearning what the world has taught us, and remembering truth. Recovery is the process of discovering who we truly are and learning how to love ourselves again. This is not so hard once we realize, we are not the person we thought we were. Sanity comes a little closer each time we are honest with ourselves and Sanity's full recovery is certainly attainable. To say we have a disease with no cure, is to say we will never be able to truly forgive ourselves; it is to say we will never be able to truly love ourselves again. This is a theory my heart will not accept.

Through this simple process of <u>willingness</u>, <u>honesty</u>, <u>forgiveness</u>, and <u>surrender</u>, all false beliefs will be exposed so that they may be replaced with truth. Your heart will always recognize truth. But without dedicated practice, it will only be forgotten again. The old saying *use it or lose it* applies here. We must continue practicing until remembering is automatic. We must learn to keep our recovery in the forefront of our thinking so that it may be in the forefront of our living.

Remember: Remembering takes practice!

Every idea we have should be carefully considered before it is put into action by simply asking ourselves the following question; "How will this affect my recovery?" Most of us are so accustomed to reacting like a short fused firecracker, that we will require continual effort in this area. Keep practicing!

The greatest shortcut in recovery is the simple decision to stop wasting time taking shortcuts

We are facing everything today. Truth and love are the same. So, if we are thinking unloving thoughts about ourselves, or about anyone else, we are indeed thinking untrue thoughts. Here we begin looking at all of our thoughts so that we may begin to break down those that are false. And how do we break down these thoughts that are anti-productive to our continued recovery? By simply recognizing them, taking responsibility for them, forgiving them, and letting them go.

Our unloving thoughts dissolve one at a time, and indeed we are set free. Our willingness becomes sure as we continue to live this new healthy lifestyle.

THE ENABLER
We must be willing to quit using our enablers.

There are enablers in the life of every addict. Most enablers think they are helping their loved one although they are not. Most enablers are unaware that they are enabling. This makes it unlikely that they will stop enabling anytime soon. We may need to cut our enablers out of our lives for some time, and some we may need to surrender for good.

Active addicts everywhere are caught up in a hustle made up of fast talk and countless lies. As the truth in their lives becomes lost, they begin to doubt it was ever real at all. There cannot be any prolonged peace in a life that is only as secure as the last lie it's told. Tireless honesty is the road back to truth.

Our illness counts on those closest to us to continue to enable us. Like the stray cat that has been fed and just won't go away, the active addict will continue to show up at the door of parents, siblings, friends; anyone who will give money, or offer a warm plate of food and some rest. What these loved ones do not realize is, when they open the door, they are indeed enabling this insane lifestyle to continue and hurting rather than healing their loved one. The enabler is always in denial and indeed part of the active addict's problem. The sooner the addict hits bottom, the better.

Sometimes people come together for no other reason than to feed their insanity and addictions. The codependent relationship, in all its unhealthy forms, always serves an insane purpose. There is always something each one thinks they can get out of the relationship or be sure they would no longer subject themselves to such abuse. Like with anything else that needs changing, when the pain gets great enough, the insane relationship will be forgiven and changed, or forgiven and let go.

In recovery we clearly see who our enablers are. It is now up to us to quit using them!

28

ALONE

Isolation is a part of addiction's insanity. Isolation has been the final straw in pushing many active addicts over the edge. In isolation, the less we step out into the sunlight, where our neighbors can see us, the less we want to. We irrationally believe that we are the topic of others' conversations. What is happening in our lives is nowhere near as important to others as our paranoid state of mind would have us believe. If you have a thought that is unloving and held onto in judgment, rather than forgiven and let go; no matter how righteous the perceived justification for holding on, it does not support recovery. Forgive that thought, and let it go now.

THERE IS ALWAYS ANOTHER WAY TO SEE IT

Although my disease wants me to believe otherwise: In recovery, I give up nothing and gain everything. In every moment, our heart is showing us a world we have forgotten. To see this vision requires our willingness to keep an open mind. An open mind is the doorway to the heart. This is the doorway to recovery. You are nowhere near as bad as you thought you were; in fact you're not bad at all. You've only made some bad choices; mistakes! And every mistake you have ever made, has brought you here, to your second chance. When you begin to see your mistakes as opportunities to learn, the judgments you have cast upon yourself will subside, and you will begin to see clearly. Our insane lies are quickly replaced with the truth our honest heart would have us see instead.

THIS IS OUR CHANCE!

The Miracle is a sigh of relief. As long as we continue to practice this Solution honestly, our lives will continue to improve.

As long as we are blaming another, we are being dishonest. We must stop blaming others now. This is our chance! As long as our problems are someone else's fault, we are powerless to fix them. But, as soon as we take full responsibility for all of our problems, we claim rightful ownership and reclaim our power. Now, we can do something about them.

If you are not yet willing to accept full responsibility for your life, you had better become willing soon. For as long as you are blaming another, you are trying to project the responsibility of where you're at in your life, onto someone else. There is no recovery in this. To be willing is as simple as the decision to be. Simply choose willingness and stop putting it off. This is yet another opportunity of a lifetime, and it can be, if you desire, the turning point you have been praying for.

Anytime someone reminds you that you have an opportunity to break free from what holds you in chains, at that precise moment, lies your greatest opportunity. Are you willing to accept this opportunity for freedom now? Or, are you going to let another one slip by like the others? Your story does not have to end the way your diseased thinking says it will. You can recover, but love can only help those who are willing to receive it.

Many who have appeared to be a much harder case than you, have broken free from their own addictions, and with concentrated awareness remain that way. Indeed, many of us are recovering, and many have been healed completely. Recovery is always available to all who seek it. Seek it now with an honest heart. To those who do, healing is inevitable. No matter how much worse you think you have it than someone else, if you are willing to keep an open mind and follow the guidance of this Soution, you will be healed.

You will regain the trust of your family, and you will again be able *to* trust. To gain trust, you must be willing to give trust. What you put into your recovery will reflect what you get out. Start living in a positive way and you will immediately begin to see positive results. This process of healing and recovery works. In all practice of giving and receiving, you will quickly learn that as you give, you are in fact, simultaneously receiving. Whether you are receiving negativity or positivity is always decided by the vibrations you are putting out. John Lennon referred to this simple law of cause and effect as "Instant Karma." Giving is always receiving. It is but a mirror, and whatever you shine in, is instantly reflected back to you. Give freely of the love within your heart without expectation of anything in return, and see it returned to you in simultaneous abundance. Continue practicing this, and you will see that it is true. Ultimately, Love is what will cure you.

Full healing does not occur overnight. Diligent effort is required. I cannot stress enough that this process must be practiced. If you are willing only to change a little, you will only experience a little change. The more willing you are to change, the more change you will see. Ask yourself what it is that you are unwilling to change, and then ask yourself *Why?*

There is no resistance in true willingness, for if we are resisting then we are not truly willing.

We have tried being kind of willing and we have even tried being mostly willing. Finally, admitting that neither of these methods has ever really worked, we now make the decision to be completely willing. Understanding that the only true willingness is complete willingness. You are either willing or you're not. Any time we catch ourselves in a state of unwillingness, we must simply stop and return our focus to being willing to do whatever it takes in order to regain our peace. A peaceful mind has no need for anesthesia.

This illness wants you to continue to believe that you are alone when in truth you are not. It is your fear based ego that wants you to believe that you have it the worst, and that your case is the hardest. However, this is not the case! It is only your unhealthy mind that wants you to accept that it's too late, that you have gone beyond the point of no return. However, you woke up this morning so it is NOT too late.

ASK

Ask from your heart when asking for help.

When you ask truth to reveal itself, mean it. What is the worst thing that could come from just asking? Maybe you are afraid, as

I was, of other people's reactions. You cannot please everyone, so stop trying. Stop holding yourself prisoner to an insane past. Forgive yourself for every mistake you've ever made, knowing that without those valuable mistakes you would not have learned these valuable lessons. Stop worrying about what others think right now and ask. Your top priority must be saving your life. Do not waste any more energy worrying about anything else because you are going to need all the energy you can get. Worry never helps. Worry will drain you of your positive energy quickly. Most of the things we waste our time worrying about never happen. So, stop concerning yourself with that which cannot be changed and focus only on that which can. Change your way of thinking and your life will follow suit. The less you worry about anything in this world, the less you suffer. Relief is available now. Ask.

Ask what's in your heart to lead you, and you will stop crying. You will even learn to laugh again. Stop entertaining your depression, and invite peace of mind instead. Give up this life consuming sickness you've been carrying around with you and return to good health. Trade in your anger for gratitude, your selfishness for selflessness, and your sadness for joy. Forgive all that you fear and rejoin Love.

Become willing to accept your own inner peace. If you choose to remain attentively honest with yourself, great rewards will continue to come. The more freedom you experience in this process, the more trust you will invest. There is nothing as reassuring as positive results to keep us motivated to continue forward in our quest for freedom from active insanity.

This is a simple process, but it will not always be an easy process. In the beginning of our healing, as well as throughout, we must keep our mind open. If we don't, we are doomed to fall back into those old familiar patterns of *repeating the same mistakes, each time expecting different results* thus losing a few more precious years, months, days, and moments that can never be recaptured. This insanity does not have to dictate our lives anymore.

INSTEAD OF POINTING FINGERS LEND A HAND

Since childhood we have been conditioned by the theories and opinions of those who surround us; by the schools and institutions we attended, by our peers and by the media. This conditioning had nothing to do with truth, or being right, but we believed that it did. All these false ideas were the seeds of our insanity and through our 'faith' in them (despite our soul's better judgment) our addiction took root.

Before I remembered who I am, I had to first experience who I am not.

Through the false beliefs and unhealthy behaviors I adopted, I became a product of the environment I was trying to drown out. I had full faith in the lie and because of this lack of awareness, delusion and denial ran ramped through my mind. I found myself chasing ineffectual remedies to try and fill the void and kill the pain. Of course none of these remedies worked.

Addiction will take you as far from truth as you can get. I desperately needed something to believe in. My unhealthy thoughts assured me that I was damaged goods. I knew I wasn't better than anyone else, and my diseased ego had me convinced that I was the worst of them all. I felt infectious. I completely identified with my addiction. My disease had taken control. I believed I was the sickest part of my insanity, and I had no compassion for myself.

LESSONS

Could I have been mistaken?

A mind caught up in the obsession and compulsion of chemical dependency cannot properly function. What I thought was truth was incorrect. Most of what I knew was just distorted misinformation, picked up, re-distorted and passed along again. Other people's perverted beliefs and unhealthy thoughts, passed along to all who will listen. It's no one's fault. However, once we recognize a mistake in this process, we must acknowledge it and learn the lesson it was sent to teach (there is always a lesson). Next, we simply forgive ourselves for falling for it, and surrender it to truth. When we do not learn the lesson a mistake was sent to teach, we are certain to repeat it until we do. This is true in the insanity of addiction and it is true in the insanity of history itself. The reason history seems to repeat itself, is because society has not yet learned the lesson.

We will learn these lessons, but when is up to us.

As the active addict tries to justify the mistakes of yesterday, the valuable lesson of today goes unseen. Our mistakes are always sent with a lesson attached; however, this lesson will never be learned by those in denial. Denial is dishonest delusion, and those who are trapped there, remain there by their own decision. In recovery, it is up to us to look closely at our mistakes and hereby see them in a different light, rather than continuing in our denial of them. Continuing in unconsciousness, we are so tangled up worrying about what's next, that we are blind to the solution that is always here now. In recovery we must learn these lessons, so that we may stop repeating our insane history.

We will not learn the lesson, if we continue to pretend we already have the answer.

Truth is, we don't know anything, and this is why our ego wants to make believe it knows everything. Our egoic disease does not want to admit that it could have ever been wrong. Even at the cost of recovering, it would rather go on being right and justified in its anger than be wrong and have peace. Self righteously pointing fingers and acting out, our ego based disease pushes on, placing blame on a world which causes it to react the way it does; all the while trying to find some sort of justification for its behavior. However, active addiction is NEVER justified.

Today I understand; when I don't like what I am seeing in the world, it is not what I am seeing than needs to be changed, but the way that I am seeing it. There is always another way to look at things. Not until we take full responsibility for our perceptions and our beliefs, will we be able to change whatever it is that needs to be changed. I am the one responsible for what I believe. This also means I have the power to change it.

When the pain becomes great enough, being right no longer matters.

Through this process we lay all blame aside, and we must accept full responsibility for where we have ended up in our lives. We must let go of our need to be right and reclaim the peace that is ours. We are committed to total self-honesty and accept that our problem is indeed our problem, and nobody else's. Only when we come to this level of acceptance will we truly begin to heal.

It does not matter if we think someone else is the cause of our unhappiness because with our willingness to surrender our need to be 'right' comes the simultaneous admission that we may have been wrong. This shift in perception is the spearhead of an authentic return to Sanity.

INTENSE HIGHS - EXTREME LOWS

Your life is yours and no one else's. It was yours to break, and it's now yours to fix

What you will be dealing with in the first few years of recovery is extremely unstable and intensely raw emotion. Sometimes you may find yourself floating on a 'pink cloud,' or laughing uncontrollably at something silly. While other times you may find yourself lashing out, or crying without reason. You will experience raw stabbing lows of despair, and extreme freeing highs that will fill you up with intense love and gratitude. You may feel compelled to express and share these extraordinary joy-filled feelings with whoever will listen and your disease may try and talk you out of it. But do not deny them, and share them while you are having them.

No longer keeping your pain bottled up, you must also share your extreme lows. Be it a close friend, a family member, a spiritual advisor, or counselor. Extreme lows express themselves as confusion, anger, blame, resentment, guilt, shame, etc. These states will sometimes reach such a boiling point that you may contemplate going back to numbing the pain. When this happens, share how you feel, and do not fall back into old unhealthy ways of coping.

In recovery all numbness will wear off. And we will have to face the destruction and hurt that has been left in its place. We will have to face our pain and every other fear we may have. This is the pain we have tried to avoid throughout our entire addiction. This is the pain that motivated us to feed our addiction the way we did. We were trying to run from ourselves by denying the truth and numbing ourselves, while suppressing our thoughts and emotions. And every time that hateful voice within our mind would start in on us again, we would try and drown it out by whatever means necessary. This is addiction's insane cycle and it is not a happy scene.

The insane idea of going back to our old way of coping is just that, insane!

Every emotional episode we find ourselves going through in recovery will indeed pass, as will the pain. These unharnessed emotional spurts will likely happen well into your first few years of recovery. However, if you continue to practice living life honestly to the very best of your ability, then these emotional spurts will occur much less than they did when you first came into this process. We are now facing life sober, and every moment is yet another opportunity to choose the choice that is needed in order to be free. This is simplicity.

If you want to attain true sustained freedom from your active addiction, you must learn some new means of coping. Today we turn and face our fear with a new commitment to living life healthy, no matter how hard it gets.

You can always come up with many reasons why you can't just change everything. These reasons are all just excuses. Reasons such as *I have to go to work or school, I have a family to support, or I don't want to embarrass my family* (just to name a few), are all cleverly disguised excuses that will keep you spiraling downward, and when you're already at the bottom, what's next but the grave? Remember, a dead man cannot pay the rent.

What our sick mind is convinced others think about us does not matter at all. Not even a little bit. It is only our thoughts that have kept us trapped in the insanity of our active addiction. And it is only these insane thoughts that will keep us there. You say you are willing to change, but are you even willing to change how you think?

The choice to get honest is the end of the lie
And not choosing this choice is the decision to die.

CHAPTER III

THE IMAGE

The Pressure to Be What We Are Not

I started running from myself for many different reasons. What others thought of me mattered. So much in fact, that it almost killed me. I spent many years building the false image that made up my lie, and wasted countless hours attempting to convince the world and myself that I really was who I pretended to be. I was selling myself short! While pretending to have all the answers and everything under control, I forgot the true-answer and lost all control.

Like most active addicts, I was unemployable. Many jobs came and went, each one doomed before it began. When the active addict loses a job, they also lose any self-worth that may have been acquired during that time. With every new job came new hope that this time, I might just get it right; that this time, I just might not embarrass myself or my family. But false hope is always short-lived.

If our paths crossed, you were meeting the sick, handmade delusion that I had constructed. The one in which I fully, but falsely believed. I spent so much time shaping this lie, that I lost touch with the truth. I was completely lost in my addiction and was considering ending my life on an almost daily basis.

My restless mind would keep me up long past the point of exhaustion, tossing and turning, until I would finally pass out. These thoughts often woke me up screaming and then, the real nightmare would begin; another day in hell. Enough was enough.

It is never too late to get honest!

I had been less than truthful with everyone, including myself. I silently lived within the confines of suicidal contemplation for two whole years before I had finally had enough suffering. I had to break my silence before I attempted to go through with it. If you are having these thoughts, you must get honest now and tell someone.

The false image gets so integrated into a life, that somehow, everything literally becomes connected to it and hence part of it. I started to wonder if truth had ever been real at all. Something drastic had to be done.

What yesterday I considered weakness, today I consider strength. The ability to ask for help when I needed it, and the humility to admit I couldn't do it alone, took every bit of strength I could muster. It wasn't until I got pushed to the very edge by my suffering, that I was ready to admit this.

You do not have to wait that long!

You do not have to wait until you are hanging from the end of a quickly unraveling strand. There is no need for you to suffer any longer than you already have, and you certainly DO NOT have to die. This is true no matter what you have come to find yourself addicted to.

Your addiction does not want you to become an honest person, for it knows that this would be its own demise. Stop believing what your insane disease is telling you. An active addict who decides NOT to get honest is in grave danger. Getting honest is not the end of your life, but the beginning of the end of your chaotic life.

40

The pain hits its peak as we hit our lowest and suddenly, none of the lies matter anymore. The importance of holding up the facade completely dissolves and the lie that was, no longer is. The choice between truth and the lie is ultimately the choice between life and death. To choose truth is to choose life, for the two are one and the same.

I was suffering in a deep depression. I was trying to run from myself and my problems through the insane method of abusing myself and pretending everything was okay when it wasn't. I had become antisocial. Even when I had to perform in a social situation, I was never truly there. I was always somewhere else in my head, just saying what needed to be said and doing what needed to be done, waiting for it to be over, so I could go back to the senseless seclusion that accompanied an overly active addiction. Life was passing me by.

I hated the lie that I thought was me, and I hated what had become of a life that had started off with so much promise. I was chest deep in quicksand and it was quickly getting harder to breathe. I was trying to live up to what I thought I had to be, in order to be accepted by others, and in doing so, I was attempting the impossible. It wasn't until I stopped pretending to be what I wasn't, that I could finally begin to see who I really was. In recovery, the false image must be let go. But to release without forgiveness first, only guarantees the strangers return.

A GENTLE INVENTORY

Go Easy on Yourself.

We must take a good look at our lie if we would have it replaced by truth. No more pretending. Simply look at your mistakes, receive their lessons, and forgive them quickly. Let go of them properly, so they do not return. Stop being so hard on yourself and continue to allow your heart to be your guide. The Solution is always the quiet thought of gentle compassion, heard just beyond the boisterous judgment of ego's anger and fear. Look for it there.

When seen correctly, our rash reactions always have a crucial lesson attached. They simply remind us of who we do not want to be. These are extremely valuable lessons that remind us to refocus and remain determined. We then forgive ourselves as many times as necessary, knowing that while we are wasting valuable energy beating ourselves up for a lesson we should be thankful for, we are being counterproductive to the Solution.

True recovery without honesty and forgiveness is impossible. Stop condemning yourself and honestly forgive!

Now ask yourself: "Am I still suffering in any area of my life?" If the answer is yes, welcome! The Solution is simple, but it's not always easy. Even pain has its purpose (to wake us up) and for this we should surely be thankful. Only you can take your journey and only you know what is really going on inside of you at any given time. Only you can truly take your own inventory. So again; how willing are you?

SEEING TRUTH BEYOND THE LIE

Simply live life being truthful.

Active addiction is a dishonest life of self-denial and destruction. Life in recovery is a journey of self-discovery and creation. One life offers peace, the other despair. Just because truth has not yet been wholly realized by part of the whole, does not mean the whole has ever been less than it is. In not believing the truth about yourself, you give credibility to all the false beliefs that you have held onto for far too long. But credibility does not always equal the truth, and just because you believe something, does not make it so.

Perception is just perception.

An incomplete whole could not exist anymore than a fraudulant truth. You have never been separate, and you have all that you need. Once you believe in the distorted perception of lack, you start looking to outside entities to fill a void that does not really exist. There is no void in love, but your faith in the void has made it feel real. This is where your suffering lived, breathed, and multiplied. If your faith has the power to do that, simply invest it somewhere else.

42

You have created an image, and it has grown out of control. Reaching in your bag of personas, having faith in each one, trying to be what your demented mind is telling you each situation calls for, instead of just being yourself. Here you lost sight of what is true. You believe these personas are you, but they are not. Self-honesty will reveal that the image has never been you.

Belief in the lie is what gives the lie life.

Addiction breeds lies. All lies have one thing in common, none of them are true. As long as we believe in the lie we have made, the suffering remains and we will want to go on numbing it. The image we hold onto will hold onto us. We are as addicted to our false image as we were to our substance of choice. And when we surrender the image, we have no need for the drug.

Lay down your lie and do it for good. Do not fold to your inner resistance, walk through it. Attachment to the image is addiction itself. It matters not what substance we are using in order to abuse ourselves, our addiction is always the result of our belief in the lie. Forgive the lie and let it go and with it will go your addiction.

OUR ILLNESS PROGRESSES

How high is your threshold for pain?

The longer our lie remains, the bigger it gets and the more it hurts. This is progression. When we walk and talk dishonestly long enough, our whole life becomes a lie. Completely possessed by our addiction's insanity, we fall deeper into identification with our illness and further from truth.

Untangling this mess, although always as simple as honestly forgiving and truly letting go, is never that easy.

Statistically speaking, there are not too many happy endings for the one who is caught in the grip of addiction. Yet, there are many happy endings for those who have chosen recovery! It does not matter which program one chooses to help them along on their journey, so long as it is one with a foundation of truth. If we are going to slow and reverse the progression of this illness, our program must be one that supports good health of the body, mind, and spirit.

DENIAL

I put on my mask, you put on yours; we'll meet somewhere in time and lie to each other. Each of us trying to outdo the other with our carefully arranged over-exaggerations. In active addiction we are allowing our lives to be led by a lie with which we continually try to deceive the world. In our addiction we are blind and in a constant state of self-deception. This is denial.

May all who are too blind, to know that they are blind, find and hit their bottoms soon.

Addiction is a parasite that enslaves its host with ruthless tactics. It is a monkey that climbed up onto our back while we were looking the other way, and has sunken its dagger-like fangs deep into our shoulder. Many of us have tried to close our eyes in denial of such horror, rather than look at it. Denial of addiction will only bring one further into addiction and denial of pain will only last until the pain gets to be too much. Eventually, the agony that comes with addiction will always catch up.

Addiction is a prison, deep in the desert of isolation, given life only by our fear of being honest. Its walls are as sound as the foundation they stand on, desert sand. A weak foundation in an insane life is actually good news! This prison is not inescapable.

When times get tough, and it seems like your brain is under attack, remember it is only the false image you've invented that holds you in chains.

In active addiction, all the parables and analogies of hell suddenly make sense. We begin to see our own lives as yet another metaphor for the fiery pit of damnation, but only until we find our escape in recovery. In recovery, all the parables and analogies of Heaven suddenly click. We now have some focus and we like what we see. We are done running. We turn and face our disease.

THE IMPOSTER

Anytime we find ourselves over-exaggerating in order to try and impress someone, or to make a situation seem bigger, better, or worse than it really is, we need to take note, refocus, and get honest again. Bad habits do not always die easily and being untruthful is just another bad habit the active addict has acquired along the way.

We will only recover to the degree that we are willing to continue in our practice of complete honesty.

Living in truth is the letting go of the entire image. Now that we know who we aren't, we are free to move forward and at long last, get to know who we truly are. We are only being reintroduced to a truth we once knew, back when life was a little bit simpler.

Complication is a dead end, turn back now!

Turn back to simplicity. It has always been here, yet forgotten by most. You will notice when you get here, there are others here with you. Here you realize that you are a part of something that you have never been apart from, and always been a part of. You remember a simpler time. A time when you were free to be exactly who you are, rather than some made up to impress persona. Recovery will prove to you that life is still simple. Trying to live up to the false image is what's complicated. Forgive and let go of your false image now.

**There has always been a knowing deep down inside
that the image was not real.
This is why living it hurt so much.**

45

Your *hurt* is trying to wake you up. Awaken and the hurt goes away. The state of suffering is a state of unawareness. Awareness does not suffer but heals.

Denial can kill an active addict, and more times than not, it will.

Denial causes blindness, even when insanity is quite obvious. You must admit to yourself that your life is out of control, whether it is because you are all strung out, or just because you cannot find happiness in your day to day life. This day is the day you can start to get well and be happy again. Which method we used to torture ourselves is unimportant; a life out of control is a life out of control. To be happy is to be healthy, and true happiness is real. Your opportunity to know this for sure, is right here and now.

TAKE ACTION NOW!

How many more times do you think you can afford to let this opportunity pass?

The window of opportunity is opened to you now. Do not pass it up. The insanity of addiction will have no problem bringing you back down to hell for a few more lifetimes if you do. If you do not make this commitment right now, then when will you? Forgive yesterday and forget about tomorrow! Right here and now is the only place and time you need be concerned with. Take a major strike against this insane imposter by committing yourself to good health and present living, no matter how sick you think you are.

Hell ends when we say it ends.

Use time and space as an advantage by putting as much time and space as you possibly can between you and whatever it is that is causing your life to be out of control. Lay down your drug of choice and do not pick up another to replace it. With this solution and the willingness to be free, everything is possible.

46

As long as I don't abuse myself now, I will never abuse myself again, because now never ends.

CHAPTER IV

RECOVERY NOW

Being committed to this process for the rest of my life was more than a little overwhelming at first. But only until I was reminded that I DO NOT have to be committed to this process for the rest of my life, but only for today. This profound reminder stayed with me because of its simplicity and the relief that it brought with it. I was no longer overwhelmed, for I knew that even I could stay committed to this new healthy lifestyle for one day. That day was today. I was not going to worry about sticking to my program tomorrow, for I have no guarantee that tomorrow will come. To waste today beating myself up for yesterday, or worrying about what may be tomorrow, is just another part of the ongoing insanity that is the lifestyle of active addiction. Today I will not worry or abuse myself in any way.

This idea was again put to the test, when I decided to quit smoking cigarettes. Smoking no longer served me or my commitment to living a clean and healthy lifestyle. Quitting cigarettes had been a long time coming. Kicking my addiction to nicotine was not easy, but it was simple. I reminded myself that I could quit anything for just one day, and that is how I did it.

Accepting recovery now is the surrendering of both the past and future. This allows us to start with a blank slate, free of regret or anxiety. There is now room for creativity and revelation. As I forgive the unforgiven and let go of yesterday, the real me is revealed. We do not have to hold on to our false image in order to be whole, but we must let go and allow ourselves to be who we are. We do this without fear of what others may think. As we freely forgive all that has happened before, and as we let go of all our concerns of what is to come, the present moment arises into our awareness and shows us what is true. We now know what it means to be present. Our suffering subsides and we come to know peace. This is happiness.

To live in today, we must be quick to forgive that which causes us pain. Anytime we catch ourselves thinking we are right about something, or arguing about anything, we must simply stop. That which is right has no need to argue. Ask yourself; "Why do I have a need to be right about this?" It is always the ego that needs to be right, while making someone else wrong. It is this same ego that has kept us abusing ourselves for so long. The ego is the false image we have made. The ego is the lie, and the lie is the root of addiction. Healing from active addiction begins with a simple commitment to honesty.

The ego is sneaky. Sometimes, even years into our recovery process, it is able to draw us into yet another unconscious reaction. As we continue to practice living healthy and aware, we will be able to catch ourselves before we react. Awareness will always be able to spot our disease coming. The more present we are, the better off we will be.

Recovery has no room for the stubborn.

When we are wrong, we must readily admit it. There is no more time to waste on silly ego games. The days of not being able to admit when we are wrong are over. Put your ego aside and when you are wrong, admit it! You are no longer expected to know everything. Admit error promptly, so that you can keep this healthy momentum moving forward in recovery.

Remain willing to let go of any idea, old or new, that does not serve the truth in your heart. Practice flexibility of both body and mind, while allowing your spirit to lead you.

We should frequently remind ourselves and each other, that an open mind is the doorway to truth. It is the flexible, open mind that forgives quickly, surrenders simply, and recovers truly. This is healing.

For the first time in our lives, instead of running, we are trying to understand and accept the truth of who we are and what this life is about. We are not here to die at the hand of our addiction. Accept this now. Remain focused in this moment, and the results will be your sure return to Sanity. The thought of who we were yesterday will only keep us trapped in yesterday. We must forgive that thought and let it go if we are to be free, for we are not today, who we were yesterday.

The thought that I will be better tomorrow, richer tomorrow, healthier tomorrow, or somehow happier tomorrow, is just another way to deny what is now. Thoughts such as these will steal our present awareness. We must remain present in order to know who we are, and again, this requires practice.

MINDFUL FOCUS

The thought of yesterday and tomorrow is the denial of truth.

This is a program of self-honesty. To be truly honest with our self, we must remain present. Staying present can be mastered through the *art of mindfulness.*

Take a direct look at your breathing. This is a great way to begin your practice of present living. Mindful breathing is an ancient Zen Buddhist technique. This technique works because, as we are mindfully watching our breath, we are focused in and on this moment. This moment is always when and where our breathing takes place. This practice is very simple yet very profound. Mindful breathing will keep you from dwelling on yesterday's should haves and tomorrow's what if's.

Practice this simple ancient art form here with me now.

While focused on your breathing, think this:
Breathing in I am forgiving, breathing out I let go.
Breathing in I am recovering, breathing out I let go.
Breathing in I am happy, breathing out I let go.
Breathing in I am grateful, breathing out I let go.

During our practice of Mindfulness, if we find ourselves thinking about worldly matters, we simply bring our focus back to our breath.

Breathing in I forgive the world, Breathing out I let go.

Breathing in… Breathing out...
Breathing in… Breathing out...
Breathing in…. Breathing out...

Mindfulness supports Recovery.

MINDFUL LIVING MINDFUL LIFE

Mindfulness always takes place in the present. This is where we want to be in order to recover.

If you are focused on the past, or what might happen later on, you are surely not present here now. With our attention focused on each mindful breath and each mindful step that we take throughout our day, we cannot help but recover. Our mind is no longer running ramped in thought. Here you will begin to see clearly and it will seem the insanity has lost its upper hand. This is because it has.

Mindful breathing can also be used to attain deep meditation. Mindful breathing is a method of sustained control. It is the pulling back on the reins of a mind that has been addicted and out of control far too long. With practice we are able to step back into the present whenever we remember to. We do this simply by bringing our focus back to our breathing. We are no longer being controlled by yesterday's addiction, and are able to be truly present. This is progress.

51

SHORTCUTS

All shortcuts are the long way home.

A virtual void has been left in place of the numbness we once called home. Where before we felt numb, we now feel empty and it hurts. The storms of early recovery had me wondering if it was really worth it. I thought, *"If it's going to hurt this bad, I might be better off numb."* However, once we break through to the other side of a storm, we realize, sticking to our program is always worth it.

How long we get rained on is always up to us.

Even when you don't think you will make it through another day with your recovery intact, you must dig in and refocus. As long as you stick to your program, these hard times will indeed come to an end. Only when you come out the other side with some Sanity restored, and your recovery stronger than ever, will you realize the storms invaluable worth.

BE THE RECOVERY

Recovery is the simple change of lifestyle from unhealthy to healthy.

We have found a way out of the constant insanity that was running our life. We are staying focused on today and have escaped from our prison of self. We have found our way out of sickness and death and our spirit is no longer buried beneath layers of substance and circumstance. We are no longer powerless and caught in the grip of our addiction, but powerful, because we are willing to do whatever it takes in order to recover.

Heaven and hell are not places we go after we die, but states of being while here on earth. Remember, not making the decision for recovery is the decision for something else. Not making the decision to change is only the decision to remain the same. We are simply re-training ourselves to live a healthy life in the awareness of now, and we will choose this new lifestyle as many times as it takes until we find ourselves living healthy without even trying. This choice cannot be made too often, and this process can never be practiced too much.

Choose recovery now, as many times as it takes, until Sanity has returned. This is self-discipline.

Recovery can be downright hard at times. Having tools is a must. It is our tools that will assist us through the storms. And indeed, there will be storms.

CHAPTER V

TOOLS

WILLINGNESS-HONESTY-FORGIVENESS-SURRENDER

Be **Willing** to do whatever it takes. Live **Honestly**; for to lie to another is to lie to yourself. **Forgive** everything; for what grudge is worth holding onto at the cost of recovery? **Surrender**; just let it go.

Do not fake it until you make it, Work it until it sticks.

The more you call upon and use these tools, the more you will be able to trust their reliability. <u>Willingness</u>, <u>honesty</u>, <u>forgiveness</u> and <u>surrender</u> are always accessible and consistent in their helpfulness. Many call out for a solution, but do not accept it when it is offered. Some ask only to avoid some stiffer penalty while planning and scheming the entire time, fixated on the unhealthy idea of the next opportunity to indulge in their insane and unhealthy behaviors. To those who remain unwilling, the self abuse goes on and on, as does the suffering. But for those who want to recover, True recovery begins here, now.

Today we must look directly at all the things we have been afraid of. We must face the fears we have never wanted to face. We must forgive our grudges. There is no need to stay mad about anything. We must forgive it and let it go. If our forgiven fear or resentment re-surfaces, it only implies that our forgiveness (even if we thought otherwise) was not true. We may have thought our forgiveness was true at the time, but the very fact that the resentment is still there, proves without question, that our forgiveness was not complete. This is no grounds to punish ourselves. Forgiveness takes practice. We simply take note, and look at *it* directly. Whatever "it" may be. Then, we just simply forgive it again. If anything causes us pain in any way, it has grounds to be forgiven. We must repeat this process as many times as it takes until it sticks.

Even many years into recovery, we can still have unhealthy thoughts. These are just thoughts. And these too can be forgiven with simplicity.

The miracle of recovery reminds us in any time of trouble that we are always allowed to change our mind. When the pain becomes too much to bear, we must simply change the way we have been think-ing. Instead of holding on, we must forgive. A grudge doesn't stand a chance against forgiveness. Grudges are distorted memories. They are sick beliefs from our past that are healed when truly forgiven.

It is never too late to change one's mind. With change of mind comes change of everything. Through forgiveness we see all things differently. The whole world changes right before our eyes. This new vision we receive, as we let go of our old distorted way of thinking and forgive. Ask yourself this; "What wouldn't I give up in order to recover? What is it I think I would not be able to let go of?" Ask yourself this truly, and then answer yourself honestly.

After we decide the pain has gotten too much to bear, we become willing to do whatever it takes, including putting our ego aside and letting go of our distorted resentments. We have now come to a point where we are ready let go of these fear-laden lies forever.

All fears are weak. Walk through them and see.

Addiction to the substances we've abused is just a side effect of this illness. Ego has no good intentions and wants us to suffer and die. This mental illness wants to kill its host and that alone proves it is insane. Why would we want to continue to allow something so unhealthy and unforgiving to lead us in our daily lives? Why would we want to continue listening to the horrible things it says, rather than forgiving and letting it go? Somewhere along our way, we have made the decision to believe in, and listen to, the unhealthy voice within us. And in doing so, we have chosen to remain in bondage. The voice that proclaims we are better than, or deserve more than another, is the same voice that has us convinced that we are less than someone else. This voice proclaims we are unworthy of love. This is the voice of the diseased ego and it manifests itself in a variety of clever disguises. In short, ego is our disease, and its foundation is unfounded fear. Walk through it.

Choose forgiveness instead!

I alone chose to humor the unhealthy, unforgiving thought system that showed me a world of injustice and pain, and I would remain here at the cost of my own freedom. A sick mind will show you a sick world. But as you begin healing, so will your perception of the world, and it won't hurt so much to exist anymore.

With the release of the lie, comes a lesser need to numb ourselves.

True honesty unwinds, undoes, and uncovers, everything that resembles untruth. You must continue to forgive and let go of these fabrications, one by one as they enter your awareness, repeating this process of forgiving and letting go; forgiving and letting go.

Please God, help me to forgive this unhealthy, dishonest thought that keeps me enslaved and in pain. Please take it from me and help me let it go.

EMOTIONS

**Life itself is the celebration, and if you think
you need to use outside substances in
order to celebrate, than you are missing the whole point.**

Life in recovery is anything but boring, so do not concern yourself with that. Make the decision right here and now, to waste no more time worrying about anything, ever. Worry is always a waste of time and will deplete us of our positive energy, leaving us exhausted, susceptible, and weak. Worry is just another form of fear, and if you're living in worry, then you are living in fear. Do not fear my friend: Try trust instead.

**I am always hardest on myself,
and the last to forgive myself.**

In early recovery my unstable emotions rose to the surface and their initial release was extremely intense. I laughed, I cried, I got mad and I learned how to forgive. I got mad again and I got to practice my forgiveness again. Because of the relief I experienced through this practice, I will forgive as many times as it takes. And when I forget to forgive, the pain will return to remind me again. I will not try and convince you that this process is going to always be easy, or that it won't be scary sometimes. But with a clear head and a true desire to live honestly, we are but again reminded that there is always another way to see any situation.

REMEMBER!

With the remembrance to forgive, what was scary before now seems laughable. As soon as we reopen our mind, the evidence begins to pour in, and as a result, instant relief from the pain and long term release from the suffering. These words are nothing more than a simple reminder, pointing us in the right direction, so that we may experience *the miracle forgiveness brings* for ourselves. Inner peace is the miracle this change in perception brings.

58

Change your life by simply changing your mind. Change everything by simply remembering to see things in another light, from another perspective. Take full responsibility for your actions. Forgive yourself and forgive all others. If you do not follow up on your decision to do whatever it takes, you will indeed stay trapped in the thought system that has brought you to your bottom. You might not want to believe that it is this simple, because you can still hear the spiteful voice of ego laughing loudly as if you were a fool to even give the thought of change, a second thought. Forgive this thought too. Any thought that attacks is not beneficial to your recovery and must be forgiven and let go immediately.

This disease will use everything in its power to try and bring us back to hopelessness. Ego will stoop to new levels of downright trickery and outright viciousness. This disease seems to think for itself and it will use as many low down tactics as it can come up with in order to try and keep us down there with it. It will unceasingly try and convince us that it couldn't possibly be as simple as just deciding, or we would have made the decision a long time ago. This disease knows that honesty is its demise, and will continue to present us with opportunities to tell exaggerated stories in order to build back up our false image. It hopes we will end up doing what we have always done. It hopes we will fall back into our unconscious state of 'rash reaction,' and resort to the methods we've always resorted to.

Ego laughs again as it convincingly declares that it's not even worth trying to recover because it is too late for us, that we have been abusing ourselves for far too long. But why would this disease put forth so much effort trying to convince us recovery won't work, when it could simply allow us to try for ourselves? Our diseased ego knows that the moment the choice has been made to live honestly; it is the beginning of its own end.

The choice to get well is the choice to get honest.

To be unhappy is to be unhealthy. To be happy is to be healthy. I am the one who has not allowed myself to be happy, so it is I who must decide otherwise. Making this choice is simple. It is sticking to this decision that is the challenge because we are so forgetful. If we would just remember how much our pain hurt the last time, we would never have to make this decision again.

In recovery, we are dedicated to living this new healthy lifestyle.

We must lay aside our unhealthy substances and behaviors. We must remember to surrender again, each time we are reminded by our suffering. As soon as we perceive a problem, the solution is available. Although we may not always recognize it at first; we can be sure it has been given. We will understand this with more clarity as we realize the answers in hindsight. Indeed the answer was here all along.

We cannot fix a problem which we are unaware of, but once we become aware, it is all a matter of willingness. Still willing?

TRUE WILLINGNESS

It is the severe emptiness of active addiction that finally introduces the active addict to their own true willingness.

Once I became willing to get honest about the unhealthy lifestyle I had been living, and the sick, suicidal ideas I had been entertaining; once I became willing to forgive everyone for everything, I began to heal. Only when I became truly willing to do whatever it took in order to regain control of my life, even if that meant giving up all control; did healing begin. This is surrender.

BE WILLING TO STAY WILLING

Remain vigilantly willing to see anything that is causing you pain, differently. There is always another way to see it. You can forgive it instead!

Recovery is the simple remembrance and acceptance of truth. In this, the lie falls to dust and blows away in the wind. Now that we have begun healing from our sick way of thinking, we can see the world in a whole new light. We now ask ourselves:

What am I willing to do in order to hold onto this gift?

Will I continue to be honest with myself and everyone, or will I allow myself to slip back into the unaware insanity that was my life before? Am I willing to continue my practice of forgiveness in every situation that calls for it, or will I remain caught in the grip of the past through my unwillingness to forgive yesterday's grudges? Am I willing to continue to assume responsibility for everything in my life, not just the achievements, but the failures as well? Am I willing to look for (and find) the valuable lesson that comes with each failure?

Here, failure is transformed into success.

Am I willing to forgive and let go of my fear and my anger, my pain and my hate? Today I must be willing to forgive and surrender all that causes me pain. A sense of gentle peace and calmness begins to replace our old, false sense of urgency and sickness.

CLARITY & BALANCE

The leveling off of our once out of control emotions occurs, and what once seemed like a ride on a runaway diesel train, has now evenly slowed into a leisurely ride on an electric streetcar.

What a Relief!

Well rested and committed to our recovery, where before the spark within us was no bigger than a pinhead, there is now a blaring light, shining brilliantly, and illuminating the tracks out front on the avenue ahead. With the slowing and steadying of our mind and our life, we continue to put these tools to good use and reap the rewards that come with them.

Happiness without inner peace is impossible. And being truly happy for the first time in such a long time, we cannot help but breathe a sigh of relief.

I cannot recover alone.

CHAPTER VI

TOOLS IN ACTION

Meetings & Gatherings

The life that comes with our second chance is inspiring. We feel the spirit of truth within us, and it is a far cry from the vacuum that once tortured our soul. You can keep this inspiration for the rest of your days by recognizing it and sharing it. Indeed, unshared inspiration goes forgotten. Therefore, the choice is always yours. The choice to share the miracle you have received is the choice to truly live your life.

There are many who are presently sharing the miracle they have received, at meetings and gatherings of all kinds worldwide. A meeting or gathering is a good place to both give and receive this miracle of healing.

Remember: A meeting/gathering is anywhere two or more come together and share in the spirit of recovery and healing.

Meetings work if you want them to. And for the one who doesn't, no meeting in the world will help. Use meetings like any other tool in your toolbox, as guided by the Truth in your heart. If your heart is telling you to go to a meeting, then go. In this process we simply remain willing to serve as our heart would have us serve. Allowing ourselves to be as Love would have us be, we are healed.

REHAB

Inpatient treatment is yet another solid cornerstone for a healthy foundation in anyone's recovery. Inpatient treatment is always a smart move; if only to remove us from our immediate, toxic environment. Many active addicts do not have health care insurance, so getting into one of these facilities is not always easy. However, if you are persistent about getting into an inpatient program, you will get in. Self-honesty will advise you if this is something you should pursue.

RECOMMITTMENT & RELEASE

I now recommit myself: I will continue to listen to my heart with an open mind. Knowing that the more I learn, the more there is that I don't know.

These tools are our new coping skills, and being able to count on them in dangerous situations is essential to our continued growth and healing. Without them, we would still be trying to cope in the precarious ways that we always have. This would be insanity, because we have already learned that those unreliable ways do not work. Honesty is essential and forgiveness is required, or surrender is not true. True forgiveness without surrender is impossible, and true surrender without forgiveness is unattainable. Both forgiveness and surrender must be present in order for us to be truly free of anything.

Because it works, we must continue repeating this process as our life situations dictate. It is essential that we continue to practice using our new tools. As we *willingly* keep bringing *honest forgiveness* and *surrender* to the table, we clearly see this miracle manifest itself in all areas of our lives and the lives of those we touch. Whereas before no one was left untouched by our insanity, today, no one who's willing is left untouched by our healing.

Recovery is first and foremost, the healing of our mind.

As our mind is healed, there is less stress on our nerves and vital organs, which in turn heals our bodies. Finally, the hole we felt deep in our soul has been filled with the only thing that could ever truly fill such a void; Self-love. Here, our guilt has been lifted.

OPTIONS

Today we are walking through our problems and never, ever, avoiding them.

We've learned there's no growth in running from our problems, so now we turn and face them all instead. Being skilled at dealing with life's difficulties depends upon our being able to stop and think before we act, or more importantly before we react. This is another great side effect that comes with working this solution. With practice, we are able to stop and register any situation, by simply stepping back and taking another look, from another angle. Seeing from this balanced vantage point, we respond with a cool head rather than with the hot one we always have. Nothing is as big-a-deal as our dis-ease would like to make it.

Again, if a situation is causing pain or anxiety, there is another way to see it. Today we perceive life through the sober eyes of forgiveness, rather than the cloudy veil of blame. As we release we are released.

Our first reaction in any delicate situation should always be to *Stop!* Now take a few deep breaths while *not reacting.* It is in this simple pause that recovery is recalled.

Without our new tools of coping we are at the mercy of this disease. The more we practice forgiving people and situations, the better we become at responding rather than reacting. Being able to stop and think first allows us options. When I react on a whim, I have no options. In recovery, having an option is essential. And with the option of doing nothing at all comes freedom.

LET LOVE BE THE JUDGE

Is it possible for me to accuse you of being *judgmental* without judging you?

When I use judgment as a tool today, I'm only judging how I feel in any given moment or situation. This is done by listening to the heart with my entire "Being" and not with my brains ego-logical ears. By allowing our Intuitive-self to run the show, we are choosing the state of peace. This is completely natural. In recovery, the only thing you should ever be judging is how you feel. If you feel uneasy about a person, place, or situation, you should leave. No anger and no condemnation. Just forgive it, let it go, and keep it moving forward.

WILLPOWER

The insanity of our illness has a mind of its own. There are many labels you can place upon it in order to try and mold it into something you have no power over. However, once you become willing to lay all blame aside and take full responsibility for all of your actions and behaviors, you take your power back. It is here that you discover you were never really powerless after all. Powerlessness, although taught as an essential admission in many recovery programs, is in reality, just another unhealthy thought. I am only as powerless as I am unwilling, and today I resolve to stay willing.

I changed my mind and everything really did change.

If you think like an addict you will live like an addict. If you begin thinking like someone in recovery, you will start seeing the world through the eyes of a recovering person. Instead of hopelessness, you will have faith. Instead of disease and sickness, you will know good health and healing. If you are looking for change, simply change your mind and change starts to transpire immediately. When I changed my mind and decided to live honestly, there was an instant change in my behavior. If I wanted to live my life honestly, I had to stop telling lies. Once I stopped telling lies, more changes came, and life began to get better.

Our thoughts and behaviors go
hand-in-hand. With the change of our
thoughts, comes an inevitable change in behavior.

We remember the world of the dishonest addict, but we no longer live there. Once lost on the rough seas of insanity, we now stand thankful on the warm sunny shores of recovery. There is always room for one more. Remain willing to forgive all resentment. To forgive is to change the mind and let go where we once held on. Who is right does not matter. We must remain willing to forgive and let go of all that don't serve our recovery. This requires the true willingness to remain forever honest with ourselves.

My willingness is my power!

I am as powerful as my willingness to admit that my old way does not work.

I am as powerful as my willingness to listen to those who know how to live free.

I am as powerful as my willingness to give up my need to be right at the cost of my peace and recovery.

I am as powerful as my willingness to reach out to a friend.

I am as powerful as my willingness to share all that has been given to me.

I am as powerful as my willingness to look inward to the heart when I'm seeking guidance.

So I ask you again, you who thought you were powerless,
How willing are you to do whatever it takes?

Are you willing to stop hanging around the same people and places you've always hung around and let go of your triggers once and for all? Our triggers are just excuses waiting to be used. And there is no such thing as a good excuse.

Exactly how willing are you to save your own life?

Our willingness is where our True-Power lies, and it proves that powerlessness is a false idea. Willingness *is* the opposite of power-lessness. True willingness, like love and like truth, will encompass all, but only to the extent that we are willing to allow it. So get willing now, and stay that way.

**If you are willing to remain willing,
you are no longer powerless.**

The monkey is dead and now we are free!
But only until the next time we forget to forgive.

CHAPTER VII

LEARNING TO FORGIVE

Forgiveness brings Freedom

The more we practice the art of forgiveness, the longer we'll remain at peace. To grasp and preserve the freedom we seek, we must retrain our mind to be happy instead of miserable. We must forgive and let go instead of holding on. Maybe there are a few who can get rid of their insane habits by clinching their fists, grinding their teeth and bearing the pain, but if you are not abusing yourself with substances, yet still holding onto resentment and fear, then how free are you? The pain hurts all the same.

Start today by forgiving yourself for yesterday.

Forgiveness is recovery. It heals the sick and restores sight to the blind. Without true forgiveness, there is no true recovery. Indeed you may be able to stop abusing yourself and stay sober awhile; maybe even for many years, but true recovery is more than that. To recover is to be healed. And to be healed, one must forgive oneself. Receive forgiveness by giving it. This is simplicity.

FORGIVE US AS WE FORGIVE

Forgive us our trespasses as we forgive those who have trespassed against us. (Matthew 6:12 / Luke 11:4)

THIS IS A COURSE IN FREEDOM
FROM ACTIVE INSANITY.

We are not the image we have created. We are not the car that we drive or the things that we own. We are not the title they gave us at work or the country in which we were born. We are not the football team we root for or the religion we were born into. We're not even the religion we've decided to convert to. We are so much more than these little descriptions and false definitions.

As soon as we define something, we limit it, and ourselves, to the definition which we have assigned it. We must stop defending our definitions of things, because there is always another way to define them. As we forgive and let go of such definitions, we become able to see the truth.

**Living with my forgiveness on my sleeve,
I am ready to let go of the reins and let Love lead the way.
My mind is finally free!**

You will remember who and what you really are as you continue to work on you. Stay <u>willing</u> to keep an <u>honest</u>-open-mind. And to <u>forgive</u> and <u>surrender</u> as the opportunities make themselves available. For this is the way this solution has been laid out for you.

All of our mistakes have valuable lessons attached. Seen correctly, they are all blessings in disguise. Why would I judge and condemn myself for a lesson that needed to be learned? How could I? You must discontinue practicing this unhealthy behavior now. And if you do catch yourself judging and condemning, simply take honest note, forgive yourself, and surrender it again.

Everyone that comes into our lives is a teacher. Today I have many teachers. I have teachers who inspire me and teachers who shock me. I have teachers who show me how I want to be and how to go about getting there, and I have teachers who show me how not to be, and what not to do. Both of these teachers bring with them very important lessons that need to be recognized. How can I be resentful towards someone who came to teach me such a crucial life lesson? Today I am thankful for all of my teachers, for in truth, they all teach the same "one" lesson.

Once we realized how important these people who teach us how not to be are, we really have no choice but to forgive every last one of them. We must forgive everyone if we are going to be able to truly forgive ourselves.

Incomplete forgiveness is incomplete recovery.

Who is it I cannot forgive and why? Our healing will equal only our willingness to forgive. Anyone we think is not worthy of our forgiveness gets a free pass to the top of the list. This does not mean we will be able to forgive everyone on the first attempt, however, the ones that are not truly forgiven will continue to show themselves to us, popping up as thoughts of anger and/or resentment, until we finally free ourselves through the art of practiced and focused forgiveness.

Side Note: Just because I have truly forgiven another, does not necessarily mean I should resume a continuing friendship with them. Recovery must always come first. If an environment is not healthy for my recovery, I simply forgive and remove myself. No anger and no grudge.

All unforgiving thoughts will keep us nailed to the very same past we're attempting to nail our offenders to. When, through resent-ment, I try and keep someone condemned to their past, I am indeed missing out on who they've become and who they are today. This unhealthy denial of what is, is just another form of self-deceit, and opposes healing completely. Only forgiveness can release us from our chains. Forgiveness is the tool that will finally allow us to maintain the freedom that this process offers.

FORGIVENESS IS KEY

Practice forgiveness with an honest heart and healing is guaranteed.

Some days I just don't want to forgive, I look at these as the days that I must. If I cannot forgive you for what you did in the past, I condemn myself to the very same past. I must forgive all resentments being held in my mind, both old and new. No resentment is too small to forgive because no matter how big or small a grudge may seem, it is equally disrupting to my peace of mind. In maintaining an honest program, all of our resentments must be looked at and forgiven. Forgive your brother and your sister for whatever you see them as guilty of. Forgive them also for what they see themselves as guilty of. Here, we are all healed of our misinterpretations. I will always take with me the healing that came with the understanding that I just might have been wrong in my harsh judgments about myself. *"I might not be such a bad person after all!"* At our core, we are in fact all good people, for the core of the heart is love. When someone who believes they are not a good person does not see agreement coming from you, but forgiveness instead, the seeds of healing have been planted. This is compassion.

Forgive now, because being *right* at the cost of inner peace, is as wrong as a man can be.

In recovery, we must look honestly at all our relationships. Those with our friends and family, and the one with our Higher Power. Here too can we examine our relationship with ourselves, to see if we are still holding ourselves prisoner to any of the mistakes we made yesterday. Am I forgiving, or am I condemning?

You too deserve your forgiveness. You deserve it as much as anyone else you have ever forgiven. Forget to forgive yourself and your release goes unknown. Imperfect forgiveness is impossible and if your grievances are not wholly forgiven, than they aren't forgiven at all.

Right now I forgive every unloving and unforgiving thought I've ever had. And I also forgive myself for having them.

True happiness is peace of mind. And only this will keep us from wanting to numb ourselves again. Only the mind that is at peace is truly free. Without peace of mind, freedom is a distorted idea, for we are all slaves to our resentments but only until they're forgiven. Break the chains that enslave by simply forgiving it all. It is here that the running stops.

If I find I cannot forgive someone for what they did twenty minutes ago, or for what they did twenty years ago, it will be impossible for me to spend any substantial time living in the present moment where freedom from active-insanity abides. Everytime an unforgiven grievance resurfaces, it brings us back to the insanity of the past, how long we stay there is always up to us as individuals.

FORGIVING OUR FEAR AND OUR ANGER

We've tried all the shortcuts around forgiveness. However forgiveness is the most direct route to full on recovery.

If I am not experiencing peace, something needs to be forgiven and let go. It's as simple as that. Whenever unrest of any kind arises into our awareness, it is yet another opportunity to practice forgiving and to continue moving forward into healing. When a grievance is finally forgiven, we know it, because we experience the peace that comes with it. Delay on this is senseless.

I am walking through my anger with forgiveness as my staff.

I like how life looks through the clear eyes of recovery. I'm even thankful for the hardheaded lessons because with me it seemed, sometimes this is how they had to be learned. I am no longer running from my anger, and I am certainly not reburying it. A reburied

75

past puts us in real danger of repeating the same mistakes and remaining trapped in the insanity for even longer. A forgiven past, allows us to remember our mistakes without judgment, so that we may retain their valuable lesson. We remember them also so that we do not repeat them again. No longer repeating the same mistakes, we can now expect different results, and the chaos subsides into peace.

The heavy stress we experienced while we couldn't bring ourselves to forgive, is now simultaneously lifted as we do.

You never have to feel that stress again. Unforgiveness has kept many an addict trying to stay numb for far too long. Forgiveness lifts the stress and the suffering subsides. With our pain gone, there is no need for anesthesia.

Without forgiveness, happiness is impossible. Without happiness, peace of mind is impossible. Without peace of mind; recovery is impossible. With forgiveness, they are all inevitable. This is the truth. Accept it and recover. If you find yourself withholding forgiveness, you have forgotten this truth. Forgive and remember. This is healing.

RELATIONSHIPS AND RESENTMENT

Forgiveness lets go, resentment holds on.

Take time to get to know your true self, and somewhere along the way, you will realize you love yourself again. You will begin treating yourself the way people who love themselves do. You will find yourself living a healthy lifestyle; eating right and exercising, quietly meditating, mindfully living, and selflessly giving, because that's what people who love themselves do. Can it really be as simple as this? It is.

In early recovery, we can easily avoid the work of recovering with yet another unhealthy relationship. We must be willing to take some time for ourselves if we expect to recover from our years of self-abuse. We must stay focused on and committed to this process, putting no-one or no-thing before it. When entering into recovery, we enter into the process of salvaging the relationships that still serve us in a healthy way, and forgiving and stepping out of those that do not.

AMENDS

Amends, like anything else in this process is simple. We don't just say we are sorry like we always have, but now we live up to these words in our behaviors and actions, showing that we truly are sorry for the pain that we have caused. We prove this by discontinuing the unhealthy behaviors that have always been the root of such pain. If we are truly sorry we must live it not just say it.

ONE HURDLE AT A TIME

We will never be given more than we can handle.

Today we are taking a look at the relationships in our life; yet another honest inventory and evaluation in order to make some decisions that need to be made. Just how healthy are our relationships and what should be done about them? This evaluation has nothing to do with who is right or wrong, but merely decides if this is a relationship worth forgiving and holding onto, or, if this relationship is one that would be better off forgiven and let go. Either way, we will forgive, because we now know this is how we regain our freedom. If we want to be free of the past we must forgive it. To refuse to forgive is to refuse to move on. And today we are moving on.

Today I accept responsibility for my role in this ridiculous ego-drama. And I will forgive and make amends wherever it is needed.

Open your mind and see what your
heart has been trying to show you all along.

CHAPTER VIII

ATTENTION ATHEISTS!

What seems to give many the most trouble forgiving, are their long-held beliefs about God. Even if you call yourself an atheist like I did, and claim not to believe in God, you still have very strong beliefs about God. You believe that God does not exist, and with a closed mind, no one can convince you otherwise.

But there is more to life than what we can see with our eyes or touch with our hands. Imagine my surprise when I found out I had God all wrong. It wasn't God I didn't believe in, but someone else's warped ideas about God that I could not accept. God is NOT what most of us have been led to believe throughout our lives.

What is the truth when it comes to God? I can attempt to explain it, but the truth about God must be experienced to be known. I can help you receive this experience for yourself by simply pointing you in the right direction. Inward…

I SOUGHT AND I FOUND

Truth will always register as true within the heart.

Today we want truth. And if it isn't truth, we are not interested. If something does not register as true within our heart, we should not accept it.

Truth has nothing to do with what we think with our brain. Today we should look only to our heart for the answers we seek. Truth always registers as true within our heart first, if only for an instant, before our logical mind gets a hold of it and tries to convince us otherwise. This usually happens so fast that we do not take notice. However, because we are changing our perception through the practice of forgiveness, and learning through mindfulness to quiet our chaotic mind, we can now catch more than a glimpse of what lies beyond.

We must now take another look at the same ideas that we would have dismissed yesterday without even a second thought. Through forgiveness we see these thoughts from another perspective, and receive their message of truth. Today we are keeping our mind open, not only to allow truth in, but to allow our illusions out.

The opportunity to recognize and receive truth is available to us the instant we become aware of how unaware we are. We must no longer allow our runaway mind to dictate our lives.

In early recovery we find ourselves questioning everything. This is good, because before, if we couldn't see it, there was no question it did not exist, and it would be automatically dismissed. This is the disfunctionality of a closed mind. With practice however, we will begin to understand that just because we cannot touch it, does not mean we cannot feel it. Just because we cannot grasp it, does not mean we cannot hold it, and just because we cannot define it, does not mean we cannot know it.

What is an atheist to do when he realizes his prayer has been answered?

WHO AM I TO SPEAK OF GOD?

**I'm someone who had no faith in God, just like you.
And if you *do* have faith, then why aren't you trusting?
Faith without trust is futile!**

80

The problem this atheist had was, when I got to the end of my rope, when I didn't think I was going to make it through another day. When I had tried practically everything, and in my mind there was nothing left to try, I fell to the floor in desperate distress and found myself calling out to a God whose nonexistence I had been preaching for years.

But why; why would this God whose nonexistence I had been preaching, want to help me? Especially after all the pain I had caused. This question fueled my search for truth.

It wasn't until several weeks later that I was reminded by a stranger of that prayer I had prayed while at the end of my rope. This is when I realized that my call had been heard. My call had indeed been answered.

In this moment, I knew I had a choice to make. I could either continue allowing my insane mind to rule my life, blocking truth out, while keeping my insanity alive, or, I could forget all that insane logic for a moment and open my mind to a new idea. That there certainly could be something I do not know about something! It was time to take a closer look.

**I can always choose later to return
to my old way of thinking.**

A TURNING-POINT

Call on Truth with heart and mind open.

Here I decided to open up instead of closing back down. I took up the practice of keeping an open mind, and now understand that whenever I call upon the love within me, the answer is already there. I may not always see the answer at first, but in hindsight, I will see that it was there all along.

Truth has always been.

Just because we cannot accurately describe what God is to one another, does not mean we cannot help each other have the experience. We point our brothers and sisters in the direction of the heart just like others did for us. We can show each other God, by showing each other compassion and love, rather than condemnation and fear. As we assist others in recognizing truth for themselves, the clouds obscuring our own vision continue to lift. All of a sudden, God makes sense.

Truth is Love and this is the Highest Power we possess.

We possess it because it is within us. To know the love within, is to be able to recognize it without. Become acquainted with this Higher Power. It comes to us in the form of our highest thought, from our highest Self and it is who we truly are. Love is always our highest state of being.

Many are turned off by the word God and this is okay. Simply find another word to replace it. Remember the word God is just a word that is used to try and describe the indescribable. The word Truth is just a word that is used to try and describe the indescribable. The word Love is just a word that is used to try and describe the indescribable. So stop trying to describe it and simply accept it into your Heart.

LET TRUTH LEAD

I sought to find Truth, and Love is what I found.

A closed mind, while attempting to defend itself from the insanity of the outside world, does so at the expense of locking itself in, turning us into its prisoner, and locking love out. This is suffering.

Quiet the mind and look inward. Open the heart and know Love. Let the heart guide you in all that you do. Continually practice calling on this new found Higher Power and then trust. Love has heard your call and Truth has answered.

In active addiction we have forgotten how to trust. But there was a time when we did know how. We can remember how to trust again. We start by simply choosing to trust, rather than choosing not to.

You are not being asked to trust anything outside of yourself, but only what registers as true within the very fiber of your Being. You are only being asked to trust what your heart shows you and tells you. You are indeed being shown hell's exit here, for truth is. Trust the Highest Power within you, and simply step out of your addiction. At this moment, you are stepping into the arms of God.

Your Higher Power is real because Truth is real.

It is easy to forgive while trusting a Higher Power. And forgiveness is the key to this simple solution. If you are having a hard time, or suffering in any way, there is something that must be forgiven. If you are having a hard time forgiving, then take a look at your trust. Start by looking at that which you feel you cannot trust. This does not mean you should just blindly trust everything. It simply means you must *trust the truth within you to judge the situation.*

If your heart tells you that someone or something is untruthful, believe the guidance you have been given. Do not condemn that which is not truth, but forgive it instead.

Do not go around arguing with everyone who does not recognize the truth as you see it; remember, we all come to truth in our own time, and in our own way. For what is within one heart is within all. And because I have become friends with the truth within mine, I can indeed introduce you to yours, for they are the same truth.

Truth is our Higher Power. We have tried everything else, and none of it worked. Today we will try trusting truth.

We must open our mind to see with our heart. We have been living within the lie, while convinced it was the truth. Unaware that we were living a lie, we suffered. And this is why we self medicated. In truth, there is no need to numb ourselves.

TODAY WE ARE FACING ALL FEARS.

Trusting does not mean you don't ask questions.

It simply means any questions we may have should be directed towards our heart. We can trust in our heart because we now see that it has always been true, even when we did not listen. Today I remain committed to this process and will surrender all impractical coaching of the insane ego-logic, by simply remembering to remain willing to trust my own heart.

The end of insanity now seems plausible. And with this new vision of pure possibility, comes an overall sense of hope. Others recognize this hope as it registers as *true* within their own heart, proving to us once again, that we truly are on the right path.

Again, pain alerts us when there is something that needs to be looked at and dealt with.

Suffering comes only from resisting what is. Pain lets us know that there is a lie that needs to be looked at, a fear that needs to be walked through, a grudge that needs forgiving, or some trust that needs re-investment. We have wasted enough time playing prisoner. The past is only a delusion that our grudges keep alive. Having been dragged by our fear long enough, we've decided it's time to let go.

Truth's awareness awaits only our invitation to enter in and repair all that is false by simply standing next to it. Invite truth in today and let go of the lie that was yesterday. Truth will continue to guide you for as long as its invitation remains open. Here we again make the decision to continue our practice. In repetition, our simple program grows in strength. We are no longer just trying to cope with life, but are now really beginning to enjoy it.

Contradiction will never register "true" to a heart that's honestly seeking. Through conditioning, we have unconsciously allowed our brains to believe contradiction, and have done so at the cost of suppressing our own awareness of truth.

Thankfully, there could never really be a contradiction in truth, for once a contradiction is introduced, truth, although always present, goes completely unseen.

To unlearn ego's logic let your heart be the judge.

For many years as an atheist, I tried to defend myself against contradiction by closing my mind to it. The problem with this method is, when we close our mind to contradiction, our mind remains closed to truth as well. A closed mind is a closed mind. We must keep our mind open in this healing process so that Love may flow through, heal us and make us whole again. From this point forward, instead of closing our mind to contradiction, we will simply look at it honestly and see how it registers. Now, able to see a lie for what it is, we understand we have no use for it. With this we do not get angry, but simply forgive the lie, forgive the liar, and let go of any resentment that may be festering.

Just because my heart won't agree with your ideas about whom and what God is, does not mean God does not exist. God is truth and truth exists. Open your mind and see for yourself.

WHAT I NEEDED

Throughout my addiction, I tried almost every avenue to lay down that which was causing my life to be out of control. All I really wanted was to stop hurting. I had become willing to try just about anything. However, I still do not want to hear about an angry and punishing God. I have already heard that story many times over, and it still does not register as truth.

What I needed was to hear how God made a real difference in someone's life. I needed to know how God saved you, because I des-perately needed saving myself. I needed to hear how God loves you, and also loves me, like *all of his children* no matter what their religion or lack thereof. I needed to hear that God was not really a He, but simply the truth. I needed to hear that God loves me still, because this is what Love does, it loves!

Only Truth can fill the void the lie has left behind.

Addiction is a lie that when left behind, will seem to leave a hole in the soul. Only Love can fill that void. I am now prepared to spend the rest of my days searching for everything that isn't truth, so that I may bring it *to* truth. Here it will be exposed for what it truly is and simply released. In other words, I am bringing all unloving, unforgiving, unhealthy thoughts that reside in my mind to my heart so they can be seen as they truly are so that they can be forgiven and let go once and for all. I'm giving it all to my Higher Power and simply letting Love be the judge. This is God, and available to all, even the atheist.

We are giving life one more go at it!

Somewhere along this way of recovery, we find ourselves making healthy choices instead of wallowing in misery. We feel our rehabilitation taking place, as our choices shift from the unhealthy (that breeds sickness and pain) to the healthy (that renews us and makes us whole again.) We are lifted from sheer exhaustion and given a new inspired energy. This is healing.

Only when I stop pretending I already know everything, will I be able to learn anything.

We are always the cause of our own pain. Love wants to heal us. I once knew God, but I forgot. I placed faith in the world that surrounded me and forgot about that which is not of this world. Truth has always still been here, I just forgot it.

BE THE SHEPHERD

To forgive is to heal and be healed.
Not to forgive is to stay sick.

Today, I am dedicated to living life healthy. Holding onto resentments is not healthy. Those who do, are not dedicated to their recovery. Life as I knew it was twisted through the eyes of active insanity. For some reason, even though I was contemplating suicide on a daily basis, it still seemed easier to remain caught up in the same insane lie I had been living.

Today I admit; I cannot win a war against my addiction. Knowing this, I refuse to fight anymore but surrender instead. My white flag is up and through my own willingness, I am turning my addiction over to recovery.

A person thinking about coming into recovery needs inspiration, not condemnation. Many know they need help, but reserve some fear about asking. No one needs another person judging them, especially during those delicate early days of recovery. Judgment only helps to reseal a closed mind that was only just beginning to open.

To those having a hard time reaching out for help; Reach out anyway.

Note to self: "Please stop judging and condemning others for what they are doing and how they are living. By doing so, you are actually pushing them further away from this simple solution. Judgment and condemnation are in direct opposition of what we are trying to do here."

COMPASSION

Do not condemn your brother by pointing out his dishonesty. But rather, forgive him and direct him to the truth you see beyond it.

Practice compassion and receive compassion. As you point another toward their truth, they point you to yours. This happens simultaneously. Truth has always known your true intentions, despite all of your bad decisions. You are not condemned but welcomed back, and free to be yourself. This is forgiveness. This is acceptance.

REMEMBER AND BE FREE

There is nothing more painful than feeling nothing at all.

Layers of shame, guilt, bad memories and nightmares, riddled with denial and doubt, which conceal the deeper levels of anger, resentment and fear: This; added to the insane comings and goings and long/hard hours kept, is in a nutshell, the chaotic life of the active addict.

87

These layers of deceit do a pretty good job at assisting us in our failure to remember for what already feels like a lifetime or two. Today, we will allow truth to push these shadowy layers in our mind up to the surface so we can look at them again, but this time in honesty, and watch them all dissapear into nothingness. Finally seeing our untruths as they really are, we are able to ask our Higher Power for assistance in forgiving and letting them all go for good.

The more you deny love throughout your years, the less you see, feel, or know anything that even resembles truth. If there is even the slightest chance that asking your Higher Power could make life a little bit easier, then why would you resist? Open your mind and ask from the heart. Do it now.

I ask you this: Who was it you were praying to that day when you reached the end of your rope? At this question's honest answer stands Truth itself.

This is the one avenue you have not yet explored in your quest for release from active addiction. Allow your heart to rise to the surface and guide you in all that you do, and you will again know what it is to be Sane. Through forgiveness, you are able to remove the layers that seem to be preventing this from happening.

As you walk through your fear and allow Love to lead you and flow through you, you will experience undeniable results and come to understand the miracle that is at hand. Again, this may not always be easy, and will indeed sometimes feel overwhelming, but only during times of forgetfulness.

Throughout the years, I have recognized the signs, yet refused to receive them. Many coincidences were pondered for an instant, only to be denied and forgotten again. I no longer ignore these signs, but am on full-alert to receive them. These same signs have been being shown to you, and still are now. Deny them no more.

With an open mind and an honest heart I will no longer ignore the signs that surround me. And as I continue to follow these signs, they continue to reveal what is true. These signs are always in conflict with what my 'logical mind' is trying to get across.

The time of living with our heads in the clouds has worn out its welcome in this story, and it's now time to live honestly and in the awareness of truth. The results cannot be denied. Every ending really is a new beginning and hells exit is at Heavens front door; Knock!

Knock and the door will be opened to you. (Matthew 7:7)

EGOLOGIC

My logic almost killed me!

It is my diseased thinking that needed to be right, and this is what kept me from God all those years. Ego would force me to go on suffering for another lifetime if it could; and it will take you with us if you let it; don't. Addiction is a leech that if left untreated, will drain its host of its energy to live. With the clarity of our new found sobriety, we can usually see our disease coming, but this does not mean it will not sneak up and surprise us from time to time. Ego is quite clever, especially when it comes at us in the form of logic. Our ego-logic already has all the answers and does not need to learn anything new. Egologic lives within the walls of our own closed mind, and the only way to know freedom, is to tear down these walls and allow truth in. Egologic will fight tooth and nail because it knows that with a forgiving heart, an open mind, and the willingness to practice; its days are ultimately numbered.

We have been fighting this unwinnable battle for far too long and now our only hope for escape is surrender. Surrender is the end of the fight. Remember; we are not surrendering to our disease, but are simply surrendering the fight and handing our addiction over to our Higher Power; Truth.

Today, we are avoiding chaos that was once unavoidable.

You must no longer hold yourself in contempt for thinking the way you once thought. Even our unloving thoughts served a purpose while they remained. They showed us who we surely did not want to be, and once we saw this, change was inevitable. Do not come down so hard on yourself when you recognize a conflict within you, for your recognition confirms you are on the right path.

Because it sees its undoing, our ego-based-illness will pull no punches when it comes to the survival of the lie. It will accuse you of being a hypocrite and a liar, immoral and insane. Our diseased ego-logic will use our mistakes and insecurities against us every chance it gets, always looking for any weakness that can be used as an entry point. The voice within you that hates you, and sees the world as chaos, *is* the voice of your fear based illness.

Recovery is the new found Voice of hope that has always been there, yet gone unheard. Recovery rings true from beyond the use-less chatter that clutters the mind's shallow surface. Open-minded, today we can clearly see we have another choice. Instead of denying the Voice that loves us, we will acknowledge and accept it. This Voice speaks gently of good health, freedom from active addiction, and true peace of mind. Suddenly, we find ourselves remembering more often, that there really is a choice to be made. Choose freedom instead of bondage. Choose love in place of fear.

BLIND FAITH

To have blind faith is to choose to trust, and to open the door to vision.

If you hadn't lacked faith that you could recover, then you'd already be recovered. In the first few days of my own recovery, I was contemplating "blind faith" and had come to the conclusion that because I could always return to my old atheistic way of thinking if I wanted; I had nothing to lose. I decided to go ahead and give this method a try. It was this decision that held the door open so that the evidence I needed could begin pouring in. With my willingness to temporarily believe in that which I could not yet see, and with my heart as the judge instead of my logic, it wasn't long before I collected enough evidence of my own so that I could no longer deny what I had found. There was a power much greater than just me alone.

The early decision to remain sincerely open minded, meant trusting a truth I had not yet recognized.

My Atheist friend, I strongly advise you to make this same decision for yourself. For no one can make it for you. Open your mind and gather your own evidence. Follow your own signs and see where they lead you. Believe only what your own heart is telling you. Stop listening to the same insane logic that you always have. Come to your own conclusion about whether or not truth is real.

Truth is the honest answer to every question ever asked. Truth is the solution to every problem. You too will go from blindness to seeing and from faithlessness to knowing.

For me, blind faith rapidly evolved into a very real understanding, and established working relationship, between myself and a Higher Power. Now, I find myself remembering to invite this Power into my awareness to work with me in all situations. The more often I remember to do this, the better. I find myself allowing my heart to guide my decision making, both big and small. Healing can be integrated into every part of your life if you allow it. It is always your Higher Power's plan that you be happy.

We are now regaining good health on a persistent basis and every little painful setback, when correctly understood, is yet another important lesson that had to be learned, and a giant leap forward in this simple yet not always easy process of remembering.

The simple wisdom beyond the worldly clutter is what we are referring to when we use the word Truth or God or Love. Truth has been given many titles, each one limiting it to something it isn't. Truth cannot ever be explained correctly, but must be experienced directly through personal revelation in order to be known. Stay open to this experience and it will be yours. When you finally know truth, you will finally know God.

QUALIFIED?

Am I qualified to talk about God, or to write about God? What exactly qualifies a man to answer questions about God? Must he be a holy man? Must he be a saint? Must he be religiously educated? Many an unschooled man has awoken to truth. There is no need to accept anything that does not ring true, and there is no need to be angry with that which you cannot accept. Simply forgive what's untrue to your heart and let it fall to the wayside with no condemnation attached. Condemnation enslaves what forgiveness sets free.

My friend, you do not have to know anything about God in order to receive Gods help. You do not need to be a member of any group or religion.

Through practiced forgiveness my mind has begun healing and I no longer want my life to end; not by suicide, and not at the hands of my addiction. Today I will remember to trust when I suffer. I do not need to be right about God, or about anything else for that matter. I just need to continue recovering by listening to the message that comes from the heart. So, am I qualified to speak or write about God? We all are! This is the miracle...

Truth is simple. It is the lie that is complicated.

CHAPTER IX

A CHAPTER CALLED TRUTH

There is no such thing as half truth because truth is whole. Try to alter truth in any way and it is no longer truth but a lie. Although there seems to be many different truths, there is truly only One Truth, and either it is, or it isn't.

TRUTH IS LIFE ETERNAL

I had to first find out what truth isn't, in order to see what it is.

The image we have fabricated has nothing to do with the truth. The active addict manufactured his illusory image to try and run from that which cannot be run from. It makes no difference how fast we run or how well we hide, eventually we must turn and face life. At this turning point, we should realize, that which we have always believed to be true, isn't. Truth is not what we thought it was, and everything we thought before, was a distorted misinterpretation seen through the eyes of active insanity and addiction. Our idea of what truth is, and what truth really is, has no resemblance whatsoever. Once we welcome life rather than denying it; once we accept what is, rather than attempting to run from it (or numb ourselves to it) we will indeed discover that truth has always been here. This is Awakening.

UNTRUTH

Untruth did not exist before man, and will cease to exist when man ceases to exist. Or when man stops lying; whichever comes first!

Untruth is manmade. It is invented by the unhappy man, by the unsatisfied man. No matter how hard I tried to convince the world that I was happy and satisfied, I was neither happy nor satisfied. I forgot it was possible to truly be happy. And I thought everyone who appeared happy, was a liar, just like me.

Even after many years of consciously practicing my program, every so often, something in the outside world seems to get its hooks into me and cause me to have a negative reaction. These negative reactions are short lived, but cause maximum amounts of pain in a minimal amount of time. I must always remember the solution is one of strict-self-honesty and to pretend I am happy when I'm not, is to be deceitful to myself. I refuse to lie to myself anymore. Pretending everything is okay when it isn't is extremely exhausting, and living this lie has already proven itself not to work for me.

Our pain shows us when we are caught up in a moment of unconscious reaction, thus helping us to become conscious. We can never fix a problem we are not conscious of. We are no longer choosing to remain in a negative mindset that if entertained for long, would easily return us back to our need to numb ourselves.

Listen with your Heart.

We come equipped with a built in truth receptor. When we are presented with truth, our heart picks up on it right away. If something doesn't feel right, it probably isn't. This is why we are forgiving and letting go of any past learning that no longer serves us. Our main focus must always be on our recovery because without it, everything else falls apart. Only believe what feels right.

I am committed to this new way of life.

Sit still in comfortable silence, to connect and align with the truth that you are. The answers you seek become clear in the stillness, and you now know what you must do.

You must remain _honest_ with your self to know freedom.
You must remain _willing_ to share, to receive.
You must keep on _forgiving_ or you'll go unforgiven.
You must _let go_, or indeed you'll be dragged.

ALL ROADS LEAD HOME

I can point you in the right direction,
but I cannot be willing for you.

Most think there are as many truths as there are people with stories, however, this is false. There is only one Truth and it either is, or it isn't. You are either living your life in the awareness of truth, or you are unaware.

You may think truth for an alcoholic or drug addict is different than truth for someone who is not addicted. This is an incorrect assumption. The active addict is living outside of the _Awareness of Truth_, but this is only his road toward awareness. There are many roads, and they all lead to the same destination. Some of these roads are winding and beautiful, with plush landscapes and scenic ocean views, while other roads are dark, steep and rocky. Rest assured that all of these roads lead us to truth. Not two truths, but One.

A PAINFUL AWAKENING

We are not who we thought ourselves to be.
We are not all those labels and beliefs.

Once again we see how incorrect we were. Only this time, we are compassionate with ourselves rather than condemning. Who we aren't, has led to the direct understanding of who we truly are. Experiencing untruth has indeed led us back to truth, and for this we should be grateful. For we all need something to come home to, and thankfully, truth remains the same.

The disease of addiction is selfish, and wants you all to itself. It does not like to share, and when it does, it does so hesitantly and resentfully. Addiction is a parasite whose main objective is to steal all of its host's self-worth, before mercilessly coming in for the kill. Unawareness of truth is the root of addiction and denial will keep you imprisoned.

I was the target of my own sick mind; both slave and punisher; prisoner and jailor. Locked deep within the confines of my closed shallow mind, I was lost. Misjudged and misunderstood, I felt outcast and separate, totally unaware that I could be free, the instant I chose freedom instead.

The false belief that I was separate from the Universe, made it hard for me to ask for the help I so greatly needed.

It was an extreme spiritual suffering (lack of awareness) that would finally release the deadbolt from my self-tortured-mind, opening it just wide enough to let some healing light in. It was here that I knew I would get well. From intense pain, hope was born. And from blind faith, true faith grew.

Layers of fear, in all its hurtful incarnations, imposed from year upon year of addiction, denial, and the false belief that I was separate from the universe, had taught me yet another valuable lesson: No matter how much I deny truth, I still cannot change it. We will not recognize the huge lessons that come from our addiction, until we finally, truly, surrender it.

Because we are not separate from all that is, we were never alone like we thought we were.

The truth will always be true. And when we try to manipulate it to make it coincide with whatever it is we are trying to convince ourselves of, it automatically becomes untrue. In believing our man made manipulations, we are living the lie and totally unaware of what is really true.

We cannot bend the truth, or tell half-truths. To try and change truth is to try and kill truth. But we cannot kill that which has eternal life, and surely Truth does. Truth stands correct. Just as it was before we arrived and tried to manipulate it.

The image we've constructed is our unawareness of truth. When we let go of our image, we clearly see what is left in its place. The image is the ego's perverted persona; a stranger with corrupted beliefs, warped and insane in all of its ways. And the facts always remain just beyond the reach of its clever, sick logic. But the pain sure did feel real when we felt it, didn't it? Again, for this we should be grateful, because if the pain did not hurt like it did, then it would not have woken us up and we'd either be dead, or still living in hell, unaware, addicted and alone.

LOVE

Love is the Source of all that is true.

Love inspires all that is creative and beautiful. Love is all that is real. How have we become so afraid to talk about love? Why do we pretend we do not feel it, when in truth we do? Why do we associate the expression of love with weakness, when to express it, is the most courageous thing we could actually do? Why do we fear love, when in reality it is the only thing that can remove all of our fears, and fix a seemingly broken world? Love repairs everything. Love heals. Love is the beginning and end of all that is, yet Love has no beginning and will never end. The mind alone cannot comprehend this, but the Heart knows it absolutely. This *is* Truth.

Love, like energy itself cannot be created nor destroyed, but can only be transformed from one form to another. Love is eternal energy that cannot ever die. Love was never born because it has always been. Love is plain and pure, extravagant and amazing, ordinary, and extraordinarily kind. Love only gives, and then gives a whole lot more. There is nothing more powerful than Love, yet Love is humble. In Love's presence, all illusion is seen as it truly is, unreal. Love is *Simple* and indeed Love is the *Solution.*

If you decide to withhold love from anyone or any situation, it is from yourself that you withhold it.
You cannot withhold love and know Love.

Still, we continue to associate love with weakness and in doing so, we have unknowingly become afraid of truth. When we feel the desire to share our love, we must share it. Love wants to flow through us because that's what energy does, it flows. In many cases, we have even become afraid to let anyone know that we feel love at all. Indeed, we have suppressed it. And in turn, this has led us to forget that we ever once knew it. Once you forget the love within your heart, you have forgotten the truth that is your Self. In this state of forgetfulness, addictions spawn, and eventually, the addict will find himself in a dark, lonely place where it seems like love isn't. Unawareness is the foundation of this illness, and all of these unloving thoughts combined are just the same unfounded belief, that one can be "separate" from the whole. One couldn't.

Thankfully, it was only our thinking that seemed to separate us, and it is the simple realization that this separation is impossible that brings us back to Sanity, and the healing of our Soul. This is recovering.

How it may seem may not be how it is.

What we believe becomes our reality, but it does not mean that it *is* reality. If your beliefs are providing an unhappy reality, you must simply choose to believe something different. Remember: Pain is a great indicator that an untruth needs to be looked at. Why do we continue to hold onto tired beliefs that have never worked for us in the first place? If they did, do you think we would have found ourselves caught up in this mess? If something no longer works for you in a positive, healthy, healing way, you must simply forgive it, forgive yourself for believing it, and surrender it again.

With our renewed commitment to Self, we can mindfully watch thoughts, rise and fall, in and out of our awareness, picking and choosing which ones do, or do not warrant faith. Observe your thoughts as they come and forgive them as they're let go. Letting your heart be the judge, simply decide which ones to accept and which ones not to. Today we must only invest our faith in ideas that are of good health and healing.

The thoughts in our mind are not truth, because they can be changed. The truth in our heart never changes.

We always have a choice rather than suffering. If the foundation you are trying to build your recovery on is that of an old and unhealthy thought system, simply choose again.

THE SURVIVOR

Knocking on deaths door and surviving can certainly put things into perspective!

When we come to realize that only love is important, we won't want to waste any more time with anything that isn't. This is Sanity. And it is *this gift* our Higher Power offers. We can let this gift fade into a distant memory, or we can keep it in the forefront of our awareness. We can allow it to lead us in all of our thoughts, words and actions, nurturing it by simply allowing it to guide us, and flow through us, while reaping its great (spiritual) rewards, or we can forget it was even offered.

To reclaim peace, we withdraw our necessity to be right and make new investments. We invest in love, instead of fear, in truth, instead of the lie. There are some who may think a little fear is good but this is not true. Fear will always keep you trapped. Love will set you free. Truth and Love are One. Indeed, they are the same.

Love is not weakness, but strength.

When I see a man who is not afraid to express the love that he has, that he feels, that he is, I do not see weakness but strength. Today, this is the man I aspire to be.

In order to fully recover, you must continue allowing your Higher Power to flow through you, never holding back any of the love that is attempting to be expressed.

Who am I to suppress it?

I must share the love if I am to remain aware of it. There can never be too much love, and unlimited as love is, there is always more than enough to go around. The more love we share, the more we receive. When we share it, we actually feel our spirit come to life within us. This is how we know if we are doing it right. If we do not feel our joyful spirit within, it is only because we have been fearful of sharing. Indeed it is because we've been holding love back.

Our spirit is Love, no matter how rotten we believe ourselves to be. We must put our judgments aside and forgive once and for all if we are truly determined to be healed. Forgiveness is the simplest route to full recovery. Forgiveness is always as simple as making a decision; the decision to forgive instead.

Our freedom is just a decision away.

Forgive what makes you suffer and see that you are free. Keep no one bound to yesterday no matter how righteous you think the cause. For your forgiveness of yesterday, is your escape from yesterday. There is no grievance worth holding onto in exchange for the peace forgiveness is offering you right now.

It is the open mind that forgives and it is the closed mind that holds a grudge.

Open your mind to forgiveness, and allow Love to flow through you and heal you and the world. There is neither peace of mind at the bottom of a bottle, nor true happiness at the bottom of a bag. Numbing ourselves did not solve our problem. Addiction has robbed us of everything important, including the trust and respect of our family and close friends. Forgiveness is the road back.

ANOTHER AWAKENING

You are a stranger to me, yet I have known you forever. In your eyes I recognize you: my brother/my sister. My fear of letting you know I feel love will no longer prevent me from seeing beyond your layers of pain to where truth shines. I see beyond the dense forest of guilt where I once spent my days, and nights, to the wide open plains where love can flow freely. Freedom is the salvation which surrender brings. Love perceived correctly, is perfect and without error, sinless and without guilt. It is an understanding of truth and the realization of Self.

True-love is fearless. True-self is sinless. God is perfect and eternal. Truth cannot help but recognize itself. Love cannot help but recognize itself. The Truth within you is the truth within me, and if something does not ring true, just forgive it. Love is the source of every healthy thought we've ever had, and it is the truth that binds us as one.

INHERENT FREEDOM

Freedom is a state of being and it is yours to claim. With practice, even the man locked down in a prison cell can find true freedom. It is simply the freedom from false-self. It is freedom from the image we've invented and believed in. It is freedom from who we thought we were, but aren't. The little self we sought salvation from, was nothing more than ego. It is only our disease we wish to be free of, and we are free when we simply choose freedom.

**My addiction has now lost its control
over my once out of control life.**

Our illness seems to have a life of its own, attacking us while we're at our weakest. It will sneak up, and then kick us while we're down. It will attempt to hold us prisoner to yesterday. It hopes to find a crack in our emotionally frail surface so that it may seep in and cause us even more damage. It wants us to put our recovery aside; to try and numb our pain once again. Our disease comes at us, trying to convince us that the freedom we seek could never be: But it is! It is possible to be free from these unloving thoughts, and it is only these thoughts that cause us unrest. Today I am turning my life over to a new master: Love.

LOVE LOVES

If you won't accept truth now, then when?

Love loves, it's what Love does! Love loves unconditionally and without question. However, it isn't until we accept love that it becomes apparent. Love forgives and Love allows. Forgiving and allowing brings freedom. Love allows me, to allow you, to be who you are, and then, Love forgives me for not wanting to allow it. Love allows me see to beyond the situation without reacting to it. Manipulation and control are traits of our disease, not Love. Love forgives and Love allows.

Being truly happy again has nothing to do with learning anything new, but unlearning the insane conditioning of the world.

Our eyes and ears may indeed deceive us, and we are not as right about things as we once believed. The door is now open for healing. To live in truth, is to have surrendered our addiction and to have forgiven our lie. Surrender means not having to fight anymore, and if you are still suffering, then you are still fighting. If you are still fighting, than it is apparent you have not surrendered. Get honest with that and surrender again.

Truth left unshared will become invisible. However, this does not mean that it has gone anywhere. Take truth and put it up on a shelf, in a closet to collect dust, and after awhile, you will forget that it is there. You will forget that it is real, and day after day, year after year, it will slowly become more of a memory until you wonder if it ever really existed at all. Eventually, you won't even wonder about truth anymore, and will be living your life from a place of fearful reaction to the world that surrounds you. It is here that addiction thrives.

Today I am sane. Still making mistakes, but learning their lessons quickly and wasting no time surrendering and moving forward in a positive way. I do not want to *wake up* when I'm laying down to die, only to realize that I let the gift that was my second chance slip away, because I forgot to laugh, or because I was too tough to cry; because I was too selfish to give someone a hug, or to cool to show love.

Imagine what is missed when we are too right to be wrong, or too logical to believe in something we cannot see. For it is when we let go of all of this logic, that the something we couldn't see, comes clearly into focus and surrounds us, until it is all we can see, in everyone and everything.

Today let us quiet our mind. Our opinions mean nothing, and our anger is never justified. Today, we will look at ourselves rather than pointing our finger at others. Here we will continue forward in healthy and honest living.

The more we learn on this simple path, the more we see there is to learn. More doors are opened as true-willingness leads, and all access is finally granted!

Are you a host to recovery, or a hostage to addiction?

CHAPTER X

HOST OR HOSTAGE?

Freedom from active addiction comes one day at a time, one step at a time, one instant at a time. I break free of one bad habit and can now see the next bad habit that has been thriving virtually unnoticed behind it. Here the process starts itself over again, each time getting a little easier than the time before. This is why it is called recovering. The less "things" I want in my life, the less I will suffer. This not only includes drugs, alcohol and gambling, but things such as money, name brands and titles. Anything I think I need in order to be happy is prime material for surrender.

When we are free of one substance, we will be presented with the next one to go. This process repeats itself many times before reaching the point where it no longer has to. As we eliminate one bad habit after another by replacing them with good ones, we experience the relief that comes along with their elimination. We actually feel ourselves healing. With help from our Higher Power, we continue to release ourselves from the chains that kept us bound for so long, and when forced to, we do it one link at a time.

Our pain is a curse while we are sleeping, however as we awaken we see, that our pain was indeed the blessing that woke us up.

In recovery, we will catch ourselves attempting to be dishonest from time to time; pretending everything is alright, when it isn't. Or, making a situation out to be bigger than it really is. Remember to stay honest, and you will remain host to your recovery.

NEW WAY TO SEE: NEW WAY TO BE

New Sight - No Fright!

Recovery is building a relationship with our Highest Self. Recovery is allowing people to be where they are in their lives, without judgment or condemnation. For when you judge another, you have indeed judged yourself. Yet, when you forgive another, you are instantly freed along with him.

The thought system of our disease is one of separation and condemnation; these, the unforgiving thoughts are all false. Forgive the ego in another, for it will only try to make the ego in you react. Continue to practice forgiveness, as the opportunities arise, and soon this response will be your only reaction.

When the lie is forgiven, the lie is let go. Remain honest and dishonesty is dead. Tap into your highest thought anytime by simply remembering to do so. Awareness is key. Truth returns to our awareness the moment we become aware of untruth. We are now uncluttering our mind of all that is of no use to us in recovery. Peace is ours.

WALKING THROUGH STORMS

Walking through our storms, we realize, what we thought was a typhoon, is just a bit of rain. This is good because we can all use a cold shower now and again!

The days of active addiction were the days of active insanity. And if we choose, they are behind us. An insane mind makes insane choices, but only until the pain becomes too much.

The prison we've constructed only appears inescapable, however it is weak. Its walls are made of self-deceit and its bars are made of fear. Fear can always be simply walked through, as can the restraints of your addiction. Only when we walk through our fear will we see it for what it is; nothing. Every fear we've ever run from has grown in strength and size, but this was only in our mind. Fear will attempt to hold us for as long as we attempt to run. We must turn and face our fear right now for it to be relinquished.

Fear is a lie. Dispose of your fear by living in truth. Fear does not stand a chance in the presence of love and will disappear when honestly looked at. Bring your lie to truth and it will be gone. Give your fear to Love and it will also be gone. God is love. Do not be afraid of your fear any longer, for it can only hurt you to the extent that you allow. To continue running from yourself is to waste more precious time and lord knows we have wasted enough!

Fearful thoughts are quickly forgiven as they arise, and the more we practice, the better we become at spotting our disease before reacting in it. We are not the sick and unhealthy thoughts that pop up into our mind, and we are not our diseased addiction like we once thought we were.

AS HOST TO RECOVERY, WE ARE FREE!

When we no longer give credibility to our fearful or unforgiving thoughts, we no longer react to them. However, if we do find ourselves caught up in reaction to something, this only means we have temporarily forgotten what is true. The moment you recognize your forgetfulness, is the instant you remember truth. This is great news because in our addiction, the first reaction to our unhealthy thinking had always been to try and drown it out. Today we have another option. We will accept only the thoughts that are healthy and that align with our recovery. We will understand there is never a need to be angry with one of our unhealthy thoughts, no matter what it is, because to do so is to make the thought real. We simply forgive, and then we are free. All storms will eventually pass and when they do, we come out the other side both stronger and wiser.

Procrastination serves us not.

It seems that the older we are when we come into this process, the harder we are on ourselves for all that wasted time. The truth is; no time has been wasted. You had to be where you were, to be where you are. Many people remain in their sickness, simply because they believe the lying voice within them that keeps telling them it's too late. Dismiss this voice again now.

We've punished ourselves enough.

Simply decide to live your life in a way that agrees with strong mental, physical, and spiritual health. Get in the habit of checking yourself on a daily basis: Did I hurt anyone today? Was I dishonest? Was I willing to do whatever it takes to recover today? Did I unconsciously react to a situation today? Did I behave in a way that was unhealthy or out of alignment with my highest form of being? Was I a host to my recovery? Am I suffering?"

Again, become _honestly_ _willing_ to _forgive_ and _let go_.

Many still believe there is no way out of their addiction. However, no addiction is too strong, and no one too far gone. There's no such thing as a hopeless case. This is our chance, a chance to really experience life; a chance to feel it all. This is our chance to know what life is really all about. An opportunity to finally feel these feelings all the way through to the other side and see what waits for us there. What waits is nothing less than a miracle, and our old way of coping is now obsolete.

Covering a lie does not make it go away. Looking at a lie through honest eyes will dissolve it completely.

Even if you are here for only one more day, live this day honestly. It is only your insane thinking, your ego, your disease, that wants you to believe that you are misunderstood, forgotten and alone. However, you are not forgotten because I am here now, remembering you. And, you are not alone because you are a part of all this; even if you refuse to believe it. And as for being misunderstood, maybe you are; but even this when seen from a different perspective, puts you in pretty damn good company!

A new life in recovery is simple and clear.

Now that you have decided to take your head out of the clouds, you may perceive how insane everything seems around you. You can clearly see what the lives of your worst critics and judges really look like. However, you must not point fingers in returned judgment, but instead forgive. Demonstrate compassion. Pass forward to them what was so freely given to you; another chance.

A NEW WORLD SURROUNDS US

When things look their darkest, and we are questioning our recovery, we must remember that we have already tried it the other way. The insane thought that life in recovery may not be worth it, is just that, another insane thought. Insane thoughts will still come and go from time to time, but because we are practicing, they won't come as often and they won't stay as long. Our unhealthy thoughts can now usually be seen a mile away, and this gives us time to think before reacting. With some work, life in recovery will not remain a bunch of blow ups followed by clean ups. We learn to respond rather than react, and this is true progress.

As host to recovery we have changed the world for the better. There is one less active addict out there living that insane lifestyle. There is one more person practicing an honest program that is willing to help and willing to go where led by the heart. As host to recovery, we are willing to serve. A shared miracle will reach further than we have ever imagined. The world is a better place!

We are still here, we are still alive, and we are now part of the Solution.

While in recovery, we are doing the things we were meant to do. We are fulfilling our purpose. We are truly *being the change we wish to see in the world*. We are being of service in our community and to humanity. We are finally at home within our own skin, expressing our talents and creating through love.

HEAL THE MIND, RETURN TO SANITY

There is only one Sane choice, which means there is really only one choice at all.

Recovery is a road paved in forgiveness. It is a road paved with love. If we are holding a grudge, whether it's towards our self or another, we are not coming from a place of recovery but from a place of sickness and insanity. The host to recovery knows it is insane not to forgive, for forgiveness is our pardon.

Fear of change is no reason to stay stuck in addiction.

It takes courage to ask for help when we need it. The courage to admit we cannot do it alone, is strength, not weakness. Imagine a fear so strong that it would hold you hostage to a life of familiar suffering, rather than allow you to take the leap into the unknown.

In recovery, it is the unknown that keeps us busy and makes this new lifestyle exciting. Willingly follow this path with an honest heart and you will never be bored again. Addiction to misery will keep us unhappy, because happiness is the unknown we fear. However, if we put our mind to it, we can remember a time when we were truly happy. Practice this process and the hostage is set free, for healing and recovery truly has found its host.

Some days, I just don't want to forgive.
These are the days that I must.

CHAPTER XI

FORGIVE AGAIN

To let go of the past without learning the lesson would be foolish. Do not dwell on your mistakes, but forgive yourself quickly. Learn your lessons without repeating your mistakes, and humbly keep this process moving forward in gratitude.

To blame is to hold a grudge.

As long as you are blaming others, you are holding yourself hostage. You may think it is "them" who do it to you, but only you can keep you trapped. Only you have the power to free yourself from the past. Do this through your forgiveness of it. Forgive the past and it is gone. Truly forgive it and it is gone for good! Let go of the blame and let go of the grudge, for it serves your recovery not. It may seem there is more than one past, his past and her past, your past and my past, but there is only one. Let it go. To attempt to keep anyone chained to their past by not forgiving them, is to hold yourself prisoner to the very same past. Finally forgive and be free.

Forgiveness is the miracle and it can be performed by anyone.

The road back to Sanity is paved in forgiveness. If you are not willing to forgive, you are not willing to be healed. Become willing now my friend.

After much extensive work on my program, I had come to realize there was one person I was forgetting in my quest to forgive all, I forgot to forgive myself. How could I forgive all that I have, and still hold such reservation in forgiving myself?

I will never forget the first time I looked in the mirror and was able to find some forgiveness for myself. It was a moment of pure mercy and unmistakable healing. In that moment I came to the understanding of what true compassion is and began to cry. In ancient Native American traditions crying has been said to be the cleansing of the soul. I know this to be true. At that moment, standing in front of my mirror, my forgiveness truly was, complete.

Through our practice of forgiving everything,
we come to see that all we are really forgiving
is our own sick judgments and meaningless opinions.

If you truly want to recover, then you have no choice; forgiving yourself is something you must do. By allowing your life to be led by only the thoughts that forgive, you are indeed guaranteed recovery.

MOMENTERY AWARENESS

Let us bring our focus back to this present moment
right now... For this is where Recovery lives.

It is only the unruly mind that is in danger of wandering off the path, because its wanderings are always in another time and place. The quiet mind is focus. When one who is struggling sees that we are no longer prisoner to our addictions and no longer holding ourselves captive to the past, they respond with hopefulness.

When we make the decision to change everything, and then put that decision into action, everything changes. We suddenly find

114

ourselves standing in a world we almost do not recognize, enjoying extended moments of peace like never before. We now know who we are and what we must do.

NEED A MIRACLE? BE THE MIRACLE.

**"There are two ways to live your life.
One is as though nothing is a miracle.
The other is as though everything is a miracle.
- Albert Einstein**

Release and relief is what comes with our *honest willingness* to practice *forgiveness* and *surrender*. Trust is the end of worry. This is healing.

We must forgive the unhealthy idea that proclaims we were dealt a bad hand or that we are owed something. We are no longer the victim, and have let go completely of the insane thought that someone or something is out to get us. The obsession to run from, numb, and punish ourselves has been lifted and gratitude has taken its place. True vision allows us to see we were never as bad as we thought we were, and it is this vision that also allows us to see the world in the same light.

Just think about the hours you have invested in running from yourself. Now simply forgive that thought too, and let it go. Again: The more time you waste beating yourself up for the time wasted, the more time that gets wasted. It is imperative we stop wasting time right now.

Everything is forgiven.

Keep sharing your recovery and you will keep recovering. Keep seeking truth within you and you will keep finding it. Stay on this new healthy path and your life will keep improving. Keep teaching the hidden lessons you have found, and more will be revealed to you. Keep loving and you will come to find: You are the love that you have been seeking. Never again will you seek to find completion somewhere outside of yourself, and never again will you try to be anything other than who you really are in order to impress. And if that doesn't impress, then nothing will.

The *host to recovery* looks at all things in life, all people,
and all situations, through the eyes of forgiveness.
It must, or healing is short-lived.

NEW YEARS DAY

Turn a new leaf over.

Now that we have some clarity, we see the world as a much different
place then when we were using and abusing. However, sometimes
it seems we are walking a fine line between optimism and
pessimism, and in any given moment, we can lean to either side.
Recovery is a tightrope, and when we are off balance, we
sometimes still tend to gravitate toward the negative side.

**"The optimist laughs to forget,
the pessimist forgets to laugh."
- Anonymous**

Every moment is a new decision. Will I live life confined or be
free? Will I remain in sickness or will I accept healing? The
decision to be whole is the choice that leads away from isolation
and separation. Ask from the heart and accept the healing when it
comes. Having faith in a Higher Power will not hurt you at all, but
will only help you tremendously.

**Reach deep into your heart and find the faith you need
today. Invest it in Truth and be free.**

Do not worry about all of your old beliefs and how much you have
preached them. Let those beliefs be gone, for they are of no benefit
to you now. If you are having a bad day, start it over immediately. Do
not wait for tomorrow to do this. Start over now and decide to live
the rest of this day in peace. Do not wait for New Year's Day to
begin your resolution. The *Solution* is now, and every day is New
Year's Day.

116

TRUST

Anytime you find yourself anxious about anything, you are not trusting. Trust must be practiced. Do you really believe your plan is better? Didn't you already try your plan over and over again? Didn't your plan already fail and bring you to your bottom? Know this: Your plan is not a better plan.

LIVING HEALTHY

We have been given the greatest gift we have ever received; *A Second Chance at Life!*

Another day, another chance to get it right. It is another chance to tell the truth, and another chance to forgive and let go of our suffering. When fear resurfaces, I know I simply lack trust, and when I find myself about to boast, I must remember to stay humble. When boredom comes knocking, I must simply refocus and recommit.

I can hold my head high for I have nothing to be ashamed of. I have forgiven myself and today, I can look them all in the eye! I am free from the chains of active addiction and this journey has just begun. I am equipped with all that I need. I have the tools, and the more I use them, the more I in trust them. I am thankful for the understanding I now hold, and for the healing I've worked so hard for.

I am bringing as many friends with me as I possibly can.

Do not be afraid to talk about this. There are many who need to hear our messages of hope. No fear, just truth. Do you understand how blessed you are to be alive? If so, then share it. Let us keep our gratitude out in the forefront. Our recovery is our resurrection.

THE ANSWER THAT ALWAYS WAS

**Freeing the mind brings a new vibrant energy
and the miraculous healing of self.**

Our need to be numb is virtually gone and we are now experiencing peace with intermittent moments of despair, rather than the other way around. We recognize this and take note as we happily continue down this health-conscious path, knowing that any despair which comes our way is only that which accompanies our forgetfulness. The instant we see we have forgotten again, we have indeed remembered again! Be *honestly willing* to *forgive* yourself again, and simply *let it go.*

**Peace will come when we accept it
because it is already here waiting to be accepted.**

The Answer can be accepted in an instant. Or, it can feel like lifetimes. This is always up to us. Rest assured, eventually, we will come back to, and accept, the original Answer. Love is the only answer. Would you be open enough to trust this is truth? Love has always been the only answer. We can deny love for as long as we desire by choosing fear or one of its attributes, but rest assured, in the end, we will all come back to Love. Why wait?

Let go of your fear and walk into the light.

The definition most of us associate with love, does not resemble True-love in any way. True-love is never selfish. True-love never gives of itself expecting something in return, not even a *thank you.* Yet True-love continues to give, and the return is always instant. Like light, True-love shines on any and all who are willing to stand within reach of its repairing rays.

118

Love holds no conditions nor recognizes flaw. It is as timeless as eternity itself yet found right here & now. Love is ready to guide, if we are willing to allow it to do so. Love knows us truly and wants us to know It. To know Love is to know truth. Forgiveness and surrender is the pathway to this recognition, which will in turn set us free from our self-condemnation, and allow us to fully recover in peace.

Forgive what needs forgiving, and surrender it now.

Love knows partial nothing, for everything Love touches must be healed wholly, or not healed at all. This is why the idea of an incurable disease is preposterous. Love heals. This is truth. And to say Love cannot heal you is to say God cannot heal you. God can. God does. God is.

The concept that anything is incurable, is just another tired idea which no longer serves us, or our purpose, here within this simple solution. Once I see myself as whole, and lacking nothing, I have no need to try and fill an illusory void with toxic substances and destructive behaviors. The solution is here, now, and it really is this simple. With the acceptance of Love, the incurable is cured.

A relapse is a slip up that reminds us where
we do not want to be.

CHAPTER XII

RELAPSE

One Step Back

I've heard it said; *we are only as sick as our secrets*. Simply stay honest with yourself and share what is going on in your life with someone you trust. Keep your process honest and keep it moving forward in a positive way. We must continue to practice trusting, and like anything else, the more we practice the easier it gets.

If you relapse, it is only because you have chosen to. There is no other honest reason. Even in recovery, not all of our choices are good ones. However, just because we made a bad choice does not mean we are not in recovery anymore. Do not let anyone tell you different. Pick yourself up, dust yourself off, get real with yourself, and refocus.

You may think you relapsed, because of this, or because of that, but you fell back because you chose to, and that is it. Do not use excuses or blame. Take responsibility for your actions immediately. You cannot fix what you do not own, so own it. Now, forgive yourself and surrender it again.

We have looked to our addictions for answers, and we have looked to the things of this world as well. Our attachments to things are addictions in and of themselves. We no longer place any importance upon such things.

To be addicted to anything is to be mentally attached to it. In truth, there is no other attachment but this. Addiction is deeply rooted in the unwell mind, and it is this that must be looked at. The answers we seek are not outside of us, and to continue to look for them there defines insanity. Relapse, if looked upon correctly, is just a step backwards; and sometimes in life you have to take a step back so you can see the whole picture.

ATTENTION!

To my brothers and sisters who have relapsed, do not turn your back on your recovery now. You are still pointed in the right direction. You have not lost all that you have worked for, but have learned yet another valuable lesson that needed be learned. Now you can teach this lesson and possibly keep someone from making the same mistake. Relapse is not mandatory.

To those who are looking for an excuse to abuse themselves again, this is not permission to do so. The "relapse lesson" has already been learned for you.

A WORD TO THE CHRONIC RELAPSER

**To relapse again and again is to continue
to choose insanity. This is not Recovery.**

The road to Sanity begins with the surrender of the lie. No one can surrender your lie for you. I found out the hard way, just how powerless I am over another's recovery. I cannot force someone else to surrender. In early recovery, I could not understand why any of my friends would want to stay chained to their addiction, at the cost of their own freedom, when I have found the way out.

Today I understand that we are all at different stages of our journey, and even our friends who are still caught up in their own addictions are going through exactly what they need to, in order to return to truth. Ultimately, we will all return to the inevitable truth. Have faith in this.

Let us pray our next bottom isn't the bottom of a casket.

We do not have to wait until we're lying down to take our last breath to surrender our lie, we can always choose to start living honestly now. If we remain honest, we will see clearly when we are not living healthy. It is here that we can simply choose again.

We must remain honest at all cost, or it *will* cost us all.

Addiction is a prison but there is an escape. Simply make the decision, then keep it. You will experience relief from your pain as you lay down your arms and throw up your empty hands, forgiving all those unhealthy thoughts and simply leaving them behind. You can always readopt any old thoughts that work for you later on, but in order to see which ones work and which ones don't, it is best to surrender them all right now.

If you keep enabling your insanity to thrive through repetitive relapse, your addiction will continue to take from you that which is most important to you. Surrender for real this time.

You must want recovery for yourself. To know that there is a way out and not take it is insane. I cannot help but think about what another cold winter is going to bring to those who are still out there caught up in the grips of insanity. Many of whom do not even know where they will be sleeping tonight. Addiction's drama is always an unhealthy one.

Grab hold of this Solution through complete surrender of your attachment to the lie you have created. Hold onto this Solution by sharing it with another. Share the truth within these words and see that what you're sharing has always been yours. I don't want to go to another friend's funeral.

Our relapse was just a bad choice.

123

Recovery requires vigilance. Remaining honest isn't always easy but it must be done. If I am not dedicated to the practice of honest, healthy living, then I am not recovering.

Thinking I can get away with something *just this once* is a really bad place for a recovering person to be. This type of thinking is not of recovery but of the sickness itself. Today, if I catch myself thinking this way, I immediately reach out and tell someone. Our personal program is only as strong as our willingness to remain honest. To bend the truth in any way is to abandon it completely. A foundation of lies is no foundation at all, but a tragedy waiting to happen.

FOR THOSE OF YOU ON MEDS

Anyone can tell a doctor what a doctor needs to hear in order to get a prescription filled. This is a program of strict self-honesty. If we are lying to our doctor, then we are lying to ourselves. Honesty is our program's foundation.

Remain vigilantly honest when taking any medication prescribed by a doctor.

If your doctor has you on meds, especially narcotic medication of any kind, you might want to have a second or third opinion. There is always a natural/holistic alternative. If you find yourself out of meds before your prescribed date, then there might be a problem. Are you working your program honestly, or are you deceiving yourself? Are you taking an honest inventory of what's going on within and without? Freedom comes one step at a time.

If you are cleaning your medicinal pot pipe like it's a crack pipe, there might be a problem!

Each time I feel like I'm being imprisoned, or enslaved, I simply begin the whole process again. Each time, the process gets a little easier than the time before. The fewer things I want in my life, the less I suffer. The less I'm attached to, the more freedom I know.

124

My own personal recovery started with the surrender of my poison of choice, and extended its reach deep into all aspects of my life. I had to surrender the entire lifestyle. I had to forgive and let go of the people, places, and the things that came with it. Cigarettes, fastfood, TV news and lotto, all had to go when their time came to go. Living unhealthy no longer worked for me. I had to let go of the lie I invented to impress a world that was unimpressed. An *honest willingness* to *forgive* and *surrender* is how I did it.

Today I find myself living an honest life, and reaping the rewards of an honest man. I can finally say I am happy and mean it. This does not mean I am 100% happy 100% of the time. What it does mean is that I'm no longer living in excess, and that which no longer serves a healthy life, is out of my life. All it took to recover was my willingness to change whatever needed to be changed, at all costs. And as it turns out, as host there's no cost, only gain.

A simple change of scenery will allow us to see that there is a world beyond our old limited perception. We stop listening to the part of our mind that tells us *we can't*, while focusing on the thought that knows that we can. We look beyond the part of our mind that is chaotic, unhealthy and sick, and into the healthy thought that is healing itself. Today, we are sharing this healing with others.

Through sharing, we allow ourselves to be nurtured back to health, by those who were sent to help us help ourselves. Our prayer has been answered and suddenly we have gone from total insanity to something that resembles freedom. Our spirit thanks us.

To my brothers and sisters who have relapsed, stop and forgive yourself now. Are you ready to end the suffering for good this time? Are you ready to leave the past in the past where it belongs? Are you ready to feel the freedom that comes with not worrying about what tomorrow may bring? You too can love yourself again.

To escape the chaotic life of addiction, simply change your mind and your world will change with it.

RESURRNDER NOW

Regroup-Refocus-Recommit

Our setbacks, if perceived correctly, always come with an invaluable lesson that may not have otherwise been learned.

Stop beating yourself up for the mistakes you have made and grab hold of this *Simple Solution*. Think of all you have learned, and how far you've come. Put your gratitude back where it belongs, out front, alongside your willingness. Thank God and push forward; there is much more to be done on this road back to Sanity and healing. Recovery is a simple rediscovery, a remembrance of truth, and it is the greatest adventure we will ever come to know. It is why we are here, and today we are committed.

So long as there remains a hopeless and desperate,
brother or sister, caught in the confines of active
addiction and despair, our purpose here remains.

CHAPTER XIII

SERVICE

You Are Qualified.

There are many that need our help, and only a few who have the experience that we now possess. We are survivors of the disease of addiction, and what we now own is priceless. This gift we've been granted must be continually shared in order to be continually realized.

Those who still struggle with their addictions are no different than those who do not. They are frightened. We must remember for ourselves, so that we may remind them. We can only truly remind them by showing them. As we face and walk through our own fears, we prove, there is nothing to be afraid of, ever. Walk through any fear and see it is not real. Reach out and help another walk through theirs, so that they too may join us in their rightful place on this road of recovery. Our purpose is to help them, which in turn, helps us. And to allow them to help us, which in turn, helps them. Indeed we are qualified. In fact, we are the only ones who are; you and I, who are learning it, by teaching it, and living it.

If my brother or sister is enduring today, the same problem I resolved yesterday, then I am plenty qualified to teach them how I did it. Our escape is at hand. I have found a way out. And now, I am reaching back in...

Active addiction is a symptom of fear. Different folks use different methods to try and avoid their own. Some ignore it in hopes that it will go away, while others deny it. Some consume themselves with shopping or work, while others go out and get themselves hooked on drugs and alcohol. No matter what method you use to try and run from your fear, the fact remains, you cannot run away from yourself. We all find ourselves running at one point or another, but the quicker we turn and face all of our fears, the sooner we will see them as they truly are. All fears are false.

Somewhere along the way, life had become a struggle. Service brings relief. Forgive another when they are having a hard time forgiving themselves, and see that you too are set free. Let them know that they are never alone, and with this you'll break free from your own struggle as well. Service is the key to happiness, and happiness is the key to recovery. When I am happy, I have no need to run.

LIFE OF MEANING

I thought life in active addiction was living, even during the times I didn't want to. I was alive, but I was not living at all. Living in fear is not living. Explore your talents and recognize your purpose. No matter who you are, there is a purpose for your life, and living an unhealthy life trapped in active addiction is not it.

We all have a purpose, even if we don't yet know it. Recovery is a gift that must be shared to be kept. I now own a gift I can share with the world. When we share our lessons learned, in order to help another who is struggling, we realize life is not just a series of meaningless, mundane scenes in our dramatic, little story. Life has meaning and so do you. Life has purpose and so do you. Know yourself and you know your purpose. This is simplicity at its finest.

Be creative and realize; You are as you were created.

The purpose we now have is grander than any we could have invented for ourselves. Healing is realized in the helping of others. Help your brother. Help your sister. See that you have helped yourself. We have taken our curse and transformed it into a blessing. How's that for a purpose? How is that for meaning?

Life in recovery suits us just fine.

Accept this new purpose and become part of this *Simple Solution*. Being where you've been; only you can help those who will be sent to you for help. Decide now that this purpose is yours because you are truly qualified. Once you have been through the insanity of active addiction and found your way out, you are amongst the qualified. Share how you did it. You do not need to have a special degree or be any sort of guru to help someone in need. Just come from a place of love, and let them know they are not alone. In recovery, we have the ability to save lives, and indeed we are qualified to do so. One moment we were hopeless tragedies and the next moment we are working with God to help save lives. This truly is a miracle.

I am my brother's and sister's savior; They are mine.

If you are truly willing, you will do whatever it takes. This means you will remain open-minded to be a part of this solution. Work with all the ideas that serve healing. Surrender all the ideas that do not. Forget all that you think you know, for it brought you to your bottom. Accept this new healthy vision, and version of you, and through practice ascend your own sickness forever. Indeed truth has been here all along.

Surrender yourself, and come to know Self.

When I accept what is, I no longer need to use drugs, alcohol, food, sex, or whatever it is that I am trying to use to temporarily escape that which cannot be escaped. Today, when untruth resurfaces, we simply take another honest look and realign with our willingness to forgive. We repeat this process as needed, and we do not become distraught if it takes many more times than many.

PAYING IT FORWARD

**Helping others to see the truth in
themselves, we see our own. This is service.**

You do have a purpose, and it is not dying at the hands of your addiction, but in helping others out of theirs. Be willing to put in as much effort remembering who you are, as you did trying to forget.

We now understand what our addiction was for. We survived so that we can share how we did it. Anyone in recovery can adopt this purpose. Turn a negative into a positive by surviving your own and helping another. Make this your purpose by sharing how you did it with those who are still stuck, but willing.

Remember: You can never force anyone to want to change their life. They must want change for themselves. Do not judge them. Allow them to be where they're at. This does not mean do not intervene if a loved one is abusing themselves, surely do. But after expressing yourself in a stern loving way, if they still insist on abusing themselves, you simply forgive and move forward. You do not have to sit by and witness the destruction of your loved one anymore, and you should not.

We must all accept recovery for ourselves. Once we start living this program in our life and people see the improvements in the quality of our living, a few of them may decide to come along. Most will not. Do not chase the unwilling, just continue to be a walking example for all eyes to see.

**We are always teaching somebody something;
even when we're all by ourselves.**

When I am alone I am teaching myself who I am, by what I am do-ing. Integrity is being honest even when no one is looking. So, what is it I am teaching myself about myself today? Am I teaching myself that I am forgiving? Am I teaching myself that I am compassionate? Am I teaching myself that I am honest and trustworthy?

131

When I find myself in a social situation, I might think that it is another I am teaching, but in truth, I am teaching myself who I am through my reaction, response, and correspondence with those around me. We are always teaching, all the time.

What is it you will teach yourself about you today?

If you come from a place of impatience or intolerance, you have forgotten the truth of who you are. Come from a place of compassion and understanding and you will see that love is what you are. Always remember, it is not up to us who receives this solution, it is only our responsibility to be an example by living it.

We are now paying forward that which we could never pay back. And as we pay it forward, we are paying it back. This is how it works. This *is* the *Solution of Simplicity*.

GRATITUDE

This is the Remedy.

It is now recommended that we stop and take a look around us. Take a look at what has transpired in our lives since we have begun this journey of recovery and healing such a short time ago. Take a look at the thoughts that are playing across the mind today as opposed to the thoughts that played there before. It is time again to acknowledge, feel, and appreciate, what has occured in our lives. We have been truly transformed and we are thankful from the bottom of our heart. This is gratitude. And we should keep it out front for all to see. For in sharing our gratitude we experience more to be grateful for.

There is something very special that happens inside when you realize you are living your purpose. A knowing deep within you, that you are accomplishing something meaningful. What can be more meaningful than helping another who is struggling? Today, we are actually doing what we set out to so. Suddenly everything makes sense; our addiction, our suffering, and the lies at the root.

It does not matter how old your addiction is, or how old you are. It doesn't matters how bad you think you are addicted, or how much worse you think you've got it than somebody else. Recovery is as simple as making the decision to live healthy and then sticking to it. Recovery is the simple choice that says: *"No matter how many days I have left on this planet, even if it is only one, I am determined to live this day right."* In recovery we are living life in honesty, forgiving all that needs forgiveness, being kind to every soul, showing compassion towards everyone, but most importantly toward ourselves.

It is time to start loving yourself again my friend. It is time to nurture yourself back to good health, while allowing yourself to be who you are. Forget all those old personas that kept you lying to yourself. Be grateful for this, another chance. Take it. Make the most of it. When you see an opportunity to help another through their problems with the solutions you have found from facing your own, do it without hesitation. Now you are living recovery, and healing is inevitable.

Share the gratitude you feel. Share it and see that it's true. Working hand in hand with God is simply working within the awareness of truth. Honesty will touch and bring improvement to all aspects of your life. Our continuing practice of compassionate forgiveness will help guide us to truth as it must.

You have wasted enough time unhappy and today you can choose to be grateful instead. Stop co-signing each other's negative and self-defeating beliefs. Point to the truth within one another instead. This gratitude lives within us all, but will go unnoticed by those who are unwilling to share. Share it and see that you own it. Share it and see this is truth.

THE CIRCLE OF HEALING

**Having a bad day in recovery?
Help another and see it is you, you have helped.**

We help ourselves, by helping others, while allowing others to help themselves by helping us. We help ourselves by sharing what we've learned. We help others find their way too, only maybe a little gentler than we've come to find our own. If I discontinue sharing the healing I've been given, I break this sacred circle.

An unshared message of recovery will not help anyone. It's only in sharing this new found freedom that we realize, what we have found is indeed as true as life itself.

**It is through the fearless sharing of love that
we prove to ourselves; we are the healers we are.**

This is what we do and this is how we do it: For each other, for ourselves, and for humanity. We help the hopeless by showing them hope, and in doing so recognize that where once we were hopeless ourselves, we now indeed have hope. We help those who cannot yet help themselves by hugging them when they need a hug, by forgiving them when they cannot forgive themselves, and by loving them when they cannot find any love for themselves. By believing in them, we help them to believe in themselves. Their soul is healed as they realize we are listening, and as they see we understand. As we help them fan their own spark of hope, all hopelessness dissolves. We are simply returning the favor by paying it forward.

Love heals everything it touches.

CHAPTER XIV

INSANITY ISN'T INCURABLE

The cure for any addiction is to simply love yourself again. Those who truly love themselves do not abuse themselves in any way. To say I have an incurable disease is to say I cannot ever truly love myself again. This would be an untrue statement. I do love myself again. Know your true Self and see that you're cured because once you know your true Self, you can't help but love yourself truly.

**"Love heals with certainty, and cures all sickness." -
A Course In Miracles**

To be cured is simply to accept Love. To accept Love is to accept healing. Let love heal you and be happy. For the truly happy have no need to punish themselves, or anybody. You can usually tell who the truly happy people are, because they are the ones smiling and taking care of themselves, not just on the outside, but just as importantly, within. Recovery really is an inside job.

But is it possible to be truly happy while living in this world, with all of its ignorance and insecurity? Is it possible to stop allowing these things to torment you, so that you won't want to return to those old sick behaviors?

I promise it's possible, just forgive and let go.

You are only tormented because you look at the world, and it seems to you that all is not as it should be. Let go of this idea. All is how it is, so that we may get to our next step. This does not mean that we do not stand up and lend a hand to help fix that which needs to be fixed; for standing up to help another *is* the next step, and even this will lead, to yet another step. To be angry with what is, is to add to the overall problem. Simply forgive what is, and be the Solution.

How did I recover? I simply surrendered.

To surrender is NOT to give up, but to simply let go. Surrender is the letting go of all that doesn't serve our good health, happiness, and well being. Peace of mind is true happiness and there is no true happiness without it. If something is causing our mind unrest; it is surely a candidate for surrender.

POISON IVY

Addiction is very much treatable and yes, it is curable.

When a child at play in the woods wanders off the path and contracts poison ivy, if he does not scratch this painfully itchy allergic reaction, and treats it with true love and care, it will go away promptly and he will be cured.

So long as the next time this child is playing in the forest, he remembers his painful lesson and avoids the ivy again, he will indeed remain cured. As long as he remembers, he will never have to go through that painful learning experience again. But if he forgets and wanders back into the ivy, he will again find himself suffering. This too holds true with addiction: So long as we remember the painful lessons we have learned, and do not pick up our insane method of destruction, we will remain cured. The moment we pick up our substance of choice, we have wandered off of the path. Hell all over again! Like poison ivy, addiction is curable. Just remember to stay on the path.

**Surrender brings freedom.
Our peace remains right where we left it.**

The feelings we have tried to avoid are there for a reason; to alert us when something's not right. Finding a way to avoid feeling our feelings will never fix the problem.

The days we remember to practice are always the easiest days.

When we finally let go of our struggle; when we finally let go of the past, we will finally feel the release that forgiveness brings. Pain is always just a thought that needs to be forgiven and through forgiveness we see it *all* as it truly is; our addiction, our world, and our self.

Surrender is an amazing paradox. When I surrender trying to un-derstand how surrender works and just forgive and let go, I gain pure understanding through the peace that it brings. Stillness of mind is the only true peace. Peace of mind is a requirement for maintaining ongoing recovery. Our new tools are available to us always, and when remembered, will bring peace to any scenario. Our tools are always accessible because of where we carry them. We only ever need recall them, in order to use them.

Continually practice this art of recovering and it will become ha-bitual. This is a far cry from the bad habits of our past. With practice this artform can be mastered and to master this art is to master one's self. The Master of self never reacts, but decides how to respond in awareness. This Mastery is what we strive for.

Permission to be happy; Granted!

As recovery dawns on our new peaceful mind, our old insane way of thinking becomes obsolete. We no longer run from our problems, but perceiving them as opportunities to grow, we eagerly and fearlessly face them. The *cure* is simply the *constant state of surrender*.

It is here we will find peace of mind. Once a situation is fully surrendered, it can no longer disturb our peace. Our sleepless nights are over.

SUSTAINED SURRENDER

**To surrender is to lay down all defenses.
So why are you still defending?**

True Surrender requires no work. It is only when we haven't truly surrendered that it seems like work. We are still battling, which means, we have not truly surrendered. As long as I am battling, I am insane, for war is crazy. It isn't until I truly surrender that the battle ends.

It is in true surrender that Sanity is recovered in full. If at any point you find yourself suffering or struggling in any way, wanting to numb or run from yourself for any reason, surrender is incomplete and the cure has been forgotten. You have indeed wandered off the path, but hopefully have yet to roll in the ivy. Forgive yourself quickly, and get back on the path.

**The *Simple Solution* is total surrender.
When I truly surrender, I fully recover.**

True surrender doesn't mean giving up everything you own. However, it means letting go of your attachment to things, and to your identification with them. True surrender is the end of addiction, and today we are surrendering all our addictions as they present themselves. Addiction is nothing more than a mental attachment secured in the undisciplined mind. With attachment comes suffering. Disciplined surrender lets go of attachments and the suffering simply comes to an end.

Without knowing, surrender was the first thing I did for myself in this process. Saving my own life moved quickly to the top of my priority list and swiftly put everything else into perspective. Nothing else mattered but saving my life. This is surrender.

Surrender was the first answer to my call for help and it still remains the same. It is answer to all suffering. Surrender of fear is the acceptance of Love. Love will forever be the answer. Love your brother, love yourself. Love your neighbor, for she is your brother. We will always come back to this Answer until it is fully remembered, accepted and applied. Surrender has always and will always be the answer. To truly surrender is to accept life as it is. It's to accept yourself as you are. Once this has occurred, so has the cure. Just remember to stay out of the ivy!

You can get to the other side of your addictions my friend. To where there is true healing and growth.

I share what I have received as I receive it. I teach what I have-learned by living it. This reinforces it for me. This is how it works and it really does work. Grab hold of my experience as well as your own. Take as much of my strength as you need, for there's plenty to spare considering where it comes from. The one Infinite spark of hope that just wouldn't burn out has blossomed and grown into the Awareness of truth. Addiction's cure is as miraculous as love itself because Love is the cure. Love will indeed heal us as we forgive and let go of all that isn't.

LOVE HAS FILLED THE VOID

My addiction was just a mistake I had made, that has now been fully corrected.

Like you, I'm not sure what is going to happen next in this crazy world of ours. I do know however, that just because the world around me is insane, doesn't mean I have to be. There is a place of peace and beauty, a place of silent shelter, for any and all who are willing.

Do not ask what truth is, but rather seek for yourself.

You too will find the love that cures, and you too will know what it means to be grateful. Simply accept and allow this love to work on you, by dropping your guard and letting it work through you. Be willing to look within in honesty, and you too will remember.

You will rejoin the truth that has never departed, and at long last recognize what has always been yours.

Be a living, breathing, walking example, of the truth you have found within you. Share the good news wherever you go by simply walking the talk. Keep a disciplined program of living self-honesty at work in your life and remember to smile and laugh every chance you get. Always practice what you teach in all aspects of life. Stay out of the poison ivy and on the right path.

**Active addiction is a war with yourself, and
when you surrender, you win!**

Addiction is extremely complicated. Recovery is the simple un-raveling of all that complication. Surrender is the end of the war and the end of all suffering. The healthy have no need for a cure. So, from this point forward be dedicated to living a healthy life. Recovery is the return to Love and the end of the insanity once and for all. The imposter is dead! The *Solution* is *Simple*.

What has taken place here is nothing short of a genuine miracle of healing. This is a day for celebration my friend; and today we celebrate in a different way: We smile!

The Beginning....

NOTES

NOTES

Printed In USA

SimplyTC & Co.

www.solutionofsimplicity.com
simplytc1969@gmail.com

www.ingramcontent.com/pod-product-compliance
Lightning Source LLC
Chambersburg PA
CBHW070809050426
42452CB00011B/1959